7-31-81

Dear Denise —

Our prayers will

follow yo[u]

May His richest +

best continue upon

you and yours is our

prayer.

Bro Wheeler[?]

"Mr Sara"

Jn - 1:1-14 — Rom - 8:1-18-ff -
Phil - 4:19 - Jas - 35
1 Sa - 40:28-31

Fight On! Fear Not!

ARTHUR JAMES MOORE

Fight On! Fear Not!

new york • *nashville* *ABINGDON PRESS*

FIGHT ON! FEAR NOT!

Copyright © 1962 by Abingdon Press

Library of Congress Catalog Card Number: 62-19133

Scripture quotations unless otherwise noted are from the
Revised Standard Version of the Bible, copyrighted 1946
and 1952 by the Division of Christian Education, National
Council of the Churches, and are used by permission.

Quotations on pages 14 and 17 are from *The Intention of
the Soul* by Hubert Simpson. Used by permission of
Hodder & Stoughton Limited.

B

SET UP, PRINTED, AND BOUND BY THE
PARTHENON PRESS, AT NASHVILLE,
TENNESSEE, UNITED STATES OF AMERICA

For more than half a century
her unfaltering faith,
her compassionate heart, and
her wise judgments have been,
for me,
a perpetual source of inspiration
and strength.

Introduction

Acceding to the insistent request of multitudes who have heard them, Arthur J. Moore has brought together for publication ten sermons under the title *FIGHT ON! FEAR NOT!*

While unremittingly stern in emphasizing the foibles and perils of these rapidly shifting days, these sermons are filled with a love and winsomeness that win the heart and respect of every hearer. They reveal the basic philosophy and fixed convictions of Bishop Moore, as wrought out upon the anvil of over fifty years of distinguished and far-reaching service as evangelist, pastor, and bishop.

Although I could easily be partisan in any appraisal of the dearest friend life has given me, I believe I can be altogether objective in evaluating his life and ministry. He has had one of the most colorful and effective careers known to any minister of this generation. He was born seventy-three years ago in South Georgia to parents poor in this world's goods, but rich in character and spiritual devotion.

In early manhood he was profoundly converted at a Methodist altar, and immediately felt and answered a call to the ministry, in which action he was urgently supported by his devoted wife. He joined the South Georgia Conference of the Methodist Episcopal Church, South, and was appointed to a rural circuit, but realizing the need for further educational advantages the Moore family moved to Oxford, Georgia, where he enrolled as a student in Emory College. Bishop Moore is blessed with a winsome personality and consuming love for his fellowman; he is "Exhibit A" of the vivid and burning story he has always told of the power of God to save and transform a life. His preaching has always been marked by decided spiritual results of a constructive and lasting nature.

In the fall of 1920 a radical change took place in the career of Arthur Moore; he was transferred to the West (now Southwest) Texas Conference and served as pastor of a great downtown church —Travis Park in San Antonio. Prior to this he had known but one objective in his ministry and that was to tell men and women of the power of God to save. Though an ordained member of an annual conference, he had never had occasion to become acquainted with the polity and administrative details of a pastorate, but when he reached San Antonio he plunged into his new and strange task with the assurance of a veteran. In this new phase of his career his responsibilities changed, but not his message. Sunday after Sunday, morning and evening, the great auditorium overflowed and the church altar was crowded as he preached the only gospel he knew— the power of God to save. For six years he occupied that commanding position, exercising an influence that dominated San Antonio in religious and civic affairs.

It was at this time that I came to know this great man. I was the pastor of another congregation in San Antonio when he came to that city with his family—a lovely wife and four children. His wife is a person of beauty, grace, and rare intellect. To quote her husband, "She is the human instrument through whom I was led to God and the one whose faith and prayers have inspired, encouraged, and sustained me all the way." Almost immediately Arthur Moore and I found in each other a rewarding fellowship; only a few months separated us in age; our temperaments and interests were congenial; the association, there begun, has never been broken. We were elevated to the episcopacy at the same time; we served together in that office for thirty years, and were then retired together.

Following his highly successful pastorate in San Antonio, he was appointed in 1926 to another historic downtown church—First Church in Birmingham, Alabama. Here he duplicated his ministry of San Antonio; great throngs attended his sermons and his influence became city and conference wide. In 1930 there came another change in the career of this man; he was elected a bishop by the General Conference of the Methodist Episcopal Church, South. An episcopal career began that was to span thirty years and take him to all parts of the world. Those were the years of the great depression, World War II and Korea, the Cold War; but they were years of great spiritual victories, the Bishop's Crusade, the Aldersgate Commemoration, and the unification of American Methodism. In all these movements Bishop Moore was a dominant figure. His first episcopal assignment was to the Pacific Coast, followed by the leadership of all the missionary activities of his church in China, Europe, and Africa. Although out of the country the major portion of his time, he yet found a way to act as president of the General Board of Missions, to lead the Bishop's Crusade, which he originated and which retired the great depression indebtedness of the board, and to serve on the Commission on Unification, which in 1939 brought the Methodist Church, the Methodist Church, South, and the Methodist Protestant Church into one—The Methodist Church. He was chief architect of the Board of Missions of this church and its first president, an office he held for twenty years. During these two decades, his superb skill and far-sighted statesmanship brought that great board into its present place of influence and leadership.

During those years the bishop made repeated visits to mission fields in all parts of the world and became the friend and confident of world leaders on every continent. He delivered the Episcopal Address to the General Conference of 1944, was elected to Phi Beta Kappa by the chapter at Emory University, was in constant demand for special sermons and addresses at home and abroad, delivered the Jarrell Lectures at Emory University and the Fondren Lectures at Southern Methodist University. As the years passed his influence increased and extended, and when he became during his last effective quadrennium the senior bishop of Methodism in years of service, he had reached a pinnacle attained by few men.

Throughout his entire career there has been one consuming and constant passion—to evangelize—and in all his utterances across the years he has never failed to witness for the faith within him.

The sermons in this volume have come from the bishop's heart and mind. They not only lift up the great verities of the Christian faith, but they have a never-failing and an undying note of hopefulness and a shout of triumph. The bishop has "seen and heard" that of which he preaches and continues to speak with an authority not his own; one that only time and experience can bring. Never has he been happier, nor has his ministry ever been more effective than during these days. He began as an evangelist; he served as pastor of great city churches; he was for a generation a distinguished bishop of his church; and now, having made full circle, he is devoting these more mature years of his life to full-time evangelism. His strength is unimpaired; there is the light of victory in his eye and the shout of triumph upon his lips.

These sermons will bless their readers as they have blessed their hearers. They constitute the credo of Arthur Moore: pastor, bishop, author, brother beloved, good minister of Jesus Christ, and always —evangelist.

A. Frank Smith, Bishop (Retired)
The Methodist Church, Houston, Texas

Foreword

Fight On! Fear Not! This may seem, to some, a strange title for a book of sermons. I have chosen it for two reasons. First, I believe that the Kingdom about which we sing and for which we work is not to come by a divine decree but out of the slow and painful strivings of those who follow Christ. Secondly, I am convinced that the sovereignty of God assures the ultimate supremacy of righteousness. Christian discipleship offers us not lighter burdens, not less of duty, but more of struggle, and pledges us more of strength. We are to follow Christ where the need is greatest. We must believe that by his power every human relation can be sanctified and every common task transfigured. The church can never save the world if it despairs of its redemption and certainly can never help it by running away from the battle.

We are to sing a song at midnight, not because of the darkness, but because we are sure the morning will appear. Christ does not take us out of the battle; he does something better. He gives us trust and triumph in the battle and promises that at the end of the struggle a friendly hand will guide us into the presence of One whose "Well done, thou good and faithful servant," will glorify the battle scars.

The sermons contained in this volume were preached to overflowing congregations as a part of a successful crusade of evangelism. They are published as they were preached to eager listeners. They do not represent scholarly accuracy or theological perfection. They seek only to reaffirm the deep conviction of my mind that there is only one safe move for the church and that is to advance. As long as the world can see the glow of the church's campfires, it will know the church is on the move and that God is with her. Every page of the New Testament seems to throb with the assurance of victory. Hope burned in the heart of Christ, and with an eye that sin had not dulled, he looked into the face of all that was dark and terrible and was hopeful for the world.

It is well that Christians carry about with them an overwhelming sense of the sins of men and the corruption of human society. No sane person would deny that these are critical times. For more than half a century war and rumors of war have impeded the forward march of the church and threatened the progress of mankind. Some are in danger of pitching their song in a minor key and surrendering to the forces of evil. Inadequate spiritual resources always spell anxiety. We need renewed assurance that Christ walks with us. Our minds must not dwell exclusively upon the perplexing problems of our time but upon the glories and excellencies of our risen and reigning Lord. We must live like those who face the morning, like those who with courage and steadfastness see the victory from afar. If our faith is strong enough, our devotion deep enough, and our courage stout enough, we will go forward with our banners flying.

There has always been before me an unattainable, ever-receding goal. My dreams and my deeds have not always matched. If one of the requirements for being a preacher were a sense of worthiness, I could never attempt another sermon. There are goals in spiritual attainment one always seeks but never fully apprehends. I have been comforted when I remembered that Christianity is not a religion that advertises human goodness, but one that proclaims God's marvelous grace and everlasting mercy.

Early in my Christian life I decided what kind of a preacher I wished to be. Like all of my ideals, this one has outrun my accomplishments, but, like a torch, it has burned steadily before the eyes of my soul for more than half a century. I have always wanted my preaching to deal with the central certainties of our faith. My prayer has been that I might be a faithful messenger of the gladdest news that ever broke upon the ears of men: Good news about the Savior and his power to forgive sin! Good news about the triumph of righteousness and the coming of the kingdom of God! Good news about the transfiguration of sorrow and the withering of the bitter roots of anxiety! Good news about the stingless death and the triumphant certainty of life after death!

I have never had a quarrel with life. Like other men, I have known loss and sorrow, the bitter and the sweet; but in it all I have steadfastly believed that all things work together for good to them that love the Lord. Looking at the angry inferno of the world's life, upon the anvil of my faith I have hammered out a sure confidence in the ultimate supremacy of righteousness. This does not mean that I think the time has come to fold our hands and sing the doxology. It does mean that the people of God must have a militant faith which makes us alive and hopeful, which girds us for battle with the evil forces; a faith which causes us to champion whatever promises to hasten the coming of the kingdom of God upon the earth.

Let us then resolve to fight on and fear not. With banners flying, let us greet the victory which is sure, knowing that Christ will lead us the whole way through. We may be children of the tempest, but triumph is our inheritance. Our faithfulness should be so apparent that we bequeath to those who follow courage, wisdom, and the

13

assurance of victory. The church should be a place where those who march with God can find their point of rallying.

> With faces darkened in the battle flame,
> Through wind, and sun, and showers of bleaching rain,
> With many a wound upon us, many a stain,
> We came with steps that faltered
> —Yet we came.

ARTHUR J. MOORE*

* My sincere thanks are expressed to Mrs. Edith B. Hill for her patient and pains-taking preparation of the manuscript. Without her efficient help this volume could not have been published.

Contents

15

God of the heights where men walk free,
Above life's lure, beyond death's sting;
Lord of all souls that rise to Thee,
White with supreme self-offering;
Thou who hast crowned the hearts that dare,
Thou who hast nerved the hands to do,
God of the heights! Give us to share
The kingdom in the valleys too.

Yet through the daily, dazing toil,
The crowding tasks of hand and brain,
Keep pure our lips, Lord Christ, from soil,
Keep pure our lives from sordid gain.
Come to the level of our days,
The lowly hours of dust and din,
And in the valley-lands upraise
Thy kingdom over self and sin.

Not ours the dawn-lit heights; and yet
Up to the hills where men walk free
We lift our eyes, lest faith forget
The Light which lighted them to Thee.
God of all heros, ours and Thine!
God of all toilers! Keep us true,
Till Love's eternal glory shine
In sunrise on the valleys too.

What We Live By

"And the rain fell, and the floods came, and the winds blew and beat upon that house, but it did not fall, because it had been founded on the rock."

—*Matt.* 7:25

The broad foundation upon which this first sermon of the present series is based and built is the brief and familiar scripture lesson found in Matt. 7:24-27. You will remember that our Savior closed his great inaugural address, which we call the Sermon on the Mount, by giving us three pairs of contrasts. The first was that of the two ways, the narrow way leading up to the shining heights of life and the broad way leading down to the abyss of destruction. The second was that of two trees, one bearing good fruit and one evil fruit, by which Jesus would teach us that conduct is always the result and the expression of character. The scripture lesson describes the third, two houses built upon different foundations and their fate in the same storm, one standing secure and the other going down into irretrievable disaster. By this contrast Jesus would remind us that the only secure and adequate and permanent foundation upon which one can build his life or a nation build its life is the word and the will of Almighty God.

In this lesson rests the scriptural authority for what I shall say about that which we live by and elements of strength in a nation's life. However much the schools of architecture may differ in their views concerning the construction and the ornamentation of a building, the one point on which all architects agree is that no building will long endure unless it is based upon an adequate and permanent foundation. One of the urgent and important questions of the hour in which we find ourselves is this question of security, this question of vitality, this question of permanency, this question of being so firmly based that the eroding forces of time will not destroy us.

It is the dominant question in the fields of business and labor, as leaders in these fields will testify. During recent days representatives of these two interrelated spheres of activity have been locked in conference rooms trying to find some foundation upon which business and labor can build so that our economic life will be peaceful and prosperous. Those who are engaged in the field of education tell us that it is the dominant question in this field. Educators are asking these days with great earnestness, "What kind of foundation must education have if our young people are to be equipped to go out to deal successfully with the mental and moral problems of these confusing times?"

I do not mind saying to you that as a churchman I think this matter of a sure foundation is the dominant question in the field of religion. Men by and large across the world are no longer concerned with our purely denominational accents. They may be precious to us, but men in and out of the churches are not greatly concerned about our peculiar denominational distinctions. What thoughtful men in the church and out of the church would like to know is whether or not the church has an authentic leadership and an adequate message for a critical and fateful season of the world's life, such as we are in today. The most important subject, I repeat, is this question of foundations, this question of permanency, this question of vitality, this question of security.

I need not tell you that the days in which we live have the fullness and significance of years and of decades. Like a marching army, we have come up to the crossroads at midnight, with all the sign boards down. No thoughtful and informed person would deny that there are realities in the present world situation with which temporizing and shallow makeshifts cannot cope. The floods are out again, and we do not seem to be prepared for them. We have a strange, sad feeling that something unusual is happening in the world or is about to happen and we do not feel ourselves quite prepared. Our civilization, if it is not tottering, is crumbling. We are driven to a fearless diagnosis of where we are, what is happening to us, and what eruptions are to come. We must discover again those intangible but nevertheless imperishable ideals by which we live.

What ideals shall we cherish? What goals shall we seek? What convictions shall we hold concerning God and man, concerning life and duty and destiny? Many problems press upon us—social, economic, political. I am not indifferent to them, but I shall leave these perplexing questions to men and women who are leaders in those fields. There are, however, certain problems that are moral and spiritual, and about them I have something to say. I read this paragraph from the pen of the late P. T. Forsyth recently:

The events of coming years will not be shaped by the deliberate acts of statesmen, but by the hidden currents, flowing continually beneath the surface of our history. In one way and one way only can we influence these hidden currents, and that is by setting in motion those forces of instruction and imagination which change opinion—the assertion of truth, the unveiling of illusion, the dissipation of hate, the enlargement of men's hearts and minds.

So when I come to discuss with you the motivating forces by which we live, I am pleading for these intangible, these imperishable values, these hidden currents that flow beneath the surface of our history, which if we follow them and yield to them will bring enlargement of men's hearts and minds.

Our future is not to be determined finally by political sagacity nor by temporal prosperity; it is not so much the reshaping of our institutions as the influencing of these hidden currents that results in the enlargement of men's hearts and minds. With that hurried preliminary word, I now lift my voice in this first sermon for three convictions, three ideals which flow beneath the surface of our history, but which nevertheless will surely shape our future.

First, *we need a revival of religion which will revitalize for us of this generation those spiritual ideals which went first into the making of this nation.* This is not a Fourth of July message, nor is it a Thanksgiving sermon, but if ever a nation was founded by faith, it was this nation. I hear people talking about the birth of America, why it came into being, and its progress; they do not impress me that they know the lesson too well. If ever a nation was founded by faith in God and in spiritual values, it was indeed this nation. In Argentina some years ago, Roger Babson the eminent economist was asked by a distinguished political leader of Buenos Aires, "Mr. Babson, why the difference between North America and South America?"

Being a guest, Mr. Babson replied, "What would you say?"

The man thoughtfully answered his own question in these words, "The men who came first to South America were seeking gold. The men who went first to North America were seeking God."

That is true, but not because he said it or because I say it. It is a fact of history like any other fact of history. This nation grew out of, was the expression of, and was organized to propagate certain spiritual truths, certain ideals.

Now I come back to my statement that if ever there was a nation founded by faith, it was this nation. You do not have to be a preacher, you do not have to be a religious fanatic, you have only to be an honest student of history to find all over the walls of this republic the handwriting of Almighty God. I need not recite history here for you know well the historical record. I had service in Belgium for twelve years, and time and again I was reminded that back in the sixteenth century William Tyndale the great English reformer came across the English Channel to Antwerp, then the seat of the printing industry, to get a new translation of the Bible printed that put the Word of God into language plain common people could understand. Tyndale was arrested and brought up to Vilvorde. This city of 25,000, located outside of Brussels, today has only one Protestant chapel in all of it and that one is Methodist. In Vilvorde Tyndale was kept in prison for a long time. One August morning in 1536 his captors led him out and strangled him to death; they burned his body at the stake and cast his ashes to the wind. The last word he said before death overtook him was, "Oh, God, open the eyes of the King of England." Within twelve months after the death of this Christian martyr in Vilvorde, this Bible had been printed, had been distributed, and was being read for the first time by the ordinary man. It had been hidden. Men had had their interpretation of the Word of God from others, but now it was open with all it had to say about the sacredness of life and the eminence of God and the deathlessness of the church.

As men read it, they said, "We must find a place in the world where we can practice these duties and enjoy these privileges." So it was that a little band of religious exiles fled from England to Holland, where they stayed eight years and did not have a very good time; the Pilgrims then crossed the Atlantic to establish the first settlement in New England. It took them twenty-three years to pay for their passage. They were blown five hundred miles off their course and landed in Massachusetts instead of Virginia, but they finally found the coast line of this nation and fell upon their knees. Then they wrote down for all subsequent history, "We are founding this state for the glory of God and the spread of the Christian religion." Out of this Book came their ideals and their convictions. They said, "We were not created to be the slaves of nations or councils. We are supposed to be free men."

It was a revival of evangelical religion in Northern Europe that created colonies on this continent. The Mayflower did not sail on its return voyage that first winter because it was believed the Pilgrims would be through with their foolish undertaking when spring came and would want to go back home, but not one of them left. When some of their members died—fifty-two the first winter—they did not put mounds on the graves. They leveled them and covered them with leaves so that the Indians would not know how many of their number had died.

What am I trying to say? This nation was not born from conquest. It was not made by men who were out for power. It was founded by God-fearing, liberty-loving men and women who had seized upon certain imperishable spiritual values and ideals. They wanted to work them out here.

Of course, the credit for the discovery of this continent must go to Christopher Columbus. He was a devout son of his church. He was a loyal subject of his king and queen, and he discovered America. I give him credit. I did not know much about Columbus until I read a thousand pages about him while I was crossing the Pacific a few years ago. I discovered he was over here more than once. About all I had known before this was what a man told me in Georgia one day.

"Did you know," he said, "that Christopher Columbus was a Democrat?"

"No," I replied. "What made him a Democrat?"

"When he started, he didn't know where he was going; when he got there, he didn't know where he was; when he got home, he didn't know where he had been; and he did it all on borrowed money." Perhaps I should not tell that story. It makes the Republicans too happy.

The colonization did not begin with Christopher Columbus. He came here in 1492, and well over a century elapsed before there was any serious effort to develop this new world. During that time the revival of Protestantism, of evangelical religion, was taking place in Northern Europe, and out of that movement with its deep spiritual convictions came these God-fearing, liberty-loving people to found a nation that was built and based upon these currents of faith and convictions about God which flow continually beneath the surface of our history.

"What are we to live by?" you ask me. "Where is our security? What kind of a foundation must we have if the flood is not to sweep us to destruction?"

My reply is: *We must have a revitalization of these imperishable ideals about God and man and duty and destiny if we are to live.*

Second: *We must restore to the seat of authority the Christian conscience.* You know that word—conscience. Or do you? It is not so well known as it used to be. It is not in as good standing as it once was—this principle within; this sense of honor that our fathers had when they shook hands in a bargain; this chart and compass and sail, all on the inside of man, that keeps him on his course,

25

whatever the wind and whatever the weather. If the conscience of the average American were Christian, intelligently Christian, it would not matter too much who was in Washington. Our ultimate strength is not in political sagacity, not in material prosperity, and not in the change of our institutions; but in these imperishable ideals of right and wrong firmly embedded in the individual home and in the individual mind.

Now something has happened to our conscience. Something has upset our set of values. We think cash is more important than character. We think dividends ought to have more attention than duty. We think it is more important to have dollars than it is to be decent. We have acquired such a sense of independence that secularism has almost dethroned our reason. We think that because we have penicillin, we do not need prayer; because we have the welfare state or something closely akin to it, we do not need salvation; and because we have psychology, we do not need spiritual values. This attitude is a sign that something has happened to these inner convictions—this faculty our fathers and mothers called the conscience.

The safety and ultimate survival of our nation depend upon the clarity and the strength of our ideals. I wrote down this conviction and pondered it. Is it true? Tell me if I am wrong. The ultimate survival of this nation does indeed depend upon the clarity and the strength and the sagacity with which we pursue our ideals. What ideals do we cherish? What convictions do we hold? What ideals are being set before us by this secular civilization? I would not sound pessimistic, but in many ways its interpretation of life would ignore and sometimes ridicule the basic Christian ideals. It is almost atmospheric. It is like a fog—this concept of ideals that either ignores or ridicules these basic beliefs. In fact you and I cannot honestly deny that there has been a catastrophic collapse of many ideals to which we once clung. Ideals which our fathers and mothers

26

believed to be indispensable we have set aside and consciously or unconsciously have put other standards in their place.

Thus we corrupt the stream of our national life. We put leaden weights about the climbing feet of our children. We do not need tranquilizers; we need a radical rediscovery of and a new relation to these imperishable ideals that must flow beneath the surface of our lives if we are to be saved.

Lord Byron wrote at the age of twenty-three: "I do not believe in revealed religion—I will have nothing to do with your immortality; we are miserable enough in this life, without the absurdity of speculating upon another."

Then thirteen years later, near the end of his life, he wrote these words:

> I am ashes where once I was fire
> And the soul in my bosom is dead,
> What I loved I now merely admire
> And my heart is as gray as my head.

I cannot be a faithful preacher without warning you that our strength, our perpetuity, our vitality lie not in more money or finer houses or faster cars but in a wholesome return to these hidden currents, to these intangible but imperishable ideals.

We have learned here in America in the last few years to cloak ugliness with nice names. When will we learn that something morally wrong cannot be made right by political action or by the approval of society? If it is wrong, it is wrong. Black is black. We are just deceiving ourselves when we think that to give it approval and to put a blue ribbon around its neck is to make it no longer ugly.

When I was a boy, a mother would point out to her growing son the town's drunkard as he staggered home to his unhappy wife and his crying children. She thought the worst calamity that could ever happen to her boy would be drunkenness. It was a sin; it was a shame. But today we do not call it drunkenness; it is alcoholism. You ask me, "Do you know that it is a disease?" I know it is a self-inflicted disease. If then it is a disease, why does the city or state license a store to sell a germ at one end of the street that makes a hospital necessary at the other end? This approach is just a part of today's shallow thinking. It illustrates how we have slipped away from the old-fashioned convictions to a new and popular acceptance of evil all in the name of being broad or something like that.

When I was a boy, stealing was stealing. It did not matter who did it—banker, burglar, or bishop. That was the only name we had for it—stealing. But we do not call it stealing anymore; we call it defalcation. Is that not the word? It is harder to spell, but it sounds so much sweeter and nicer than stealing.

We are thinking about a revival. A revival is more than singing hymns and hearing a sermon. It is lifting the moral and spiritual convictions of the church and of the community to a perceptibly higher level than they were. It is the re-examination of what we honestly believe about God and life and duty which should lead to a tenacious loyalty to those convictions which will dominate us more than place and property and progress.

We had a wayward boy in our state who got into trouble and went to prison. On his return, he came back to his church to give this testimony, "Well, I did go to prison, but thank God, I didn't lose my religion." The point is, when does a man lose his religion? We tend to make religion a formality of one hour on Sunday morning. We have compartmented life. The revival I am interested in will restore to us the clarity and the tenacity of our faith until it becomes a vital force by which to live, not a formality to be accepted or rejected.

Third, I have sought throughout this message to impress upon you my honest belief that *the destiny of this nation and of this world is bound up with a revival of spiritual religion.* By a revival I mean something infinitely more than a few days of preaching. I am talking about an invasion of God's spirit that will restore to us the consciousness of God and give us a sense of our responsibilities to him. What I seek to emphasize in this first sermon is that religion, spiritual religion, is the chief factor in a man's life and the most potent power in a nation's vitality. It is not a luxury that we can accept or reject. A revival of spiritual religion is the most desperate necessity of our time.

Nations do not die from attack from without. They may be overrun; they may be held in subjection. My beloved little Czechoslovakia, where I served for years and had many happy associations, was a democracy overrun, not once but twice. During the Middle Ages John Huss, the noted Protestant reformer, gave to his native Bohemia the great doctrine that all men are equal before God. On the Protestant side during the Reformation, the people were suppressed and were put to death. For three hundred years the Czechs were tied to the chariot wheels of the Austro-Hungarian Empire, and it seemed that the Czech nationality had disappeared. When Woodrow Wilson stood at the peace table and said Bohemia must be re-created, Czechoslovakia was formed, and my friend, the honored Doctor Tomas Masaryk, the great Protestant first president, was brought to power. Within twelve months after the government was born, there was a church with five thousand members in that newly created country. For three hundred years the Czechs had been under the tyrant's heel. Nations do not die permanently because of an attack from without. Nations die only when they commit suicide.

A nation begins to die at its heart when its values are upside down, when its conscience is atrophied, when its ideals are put in cold storage. We have a form of polite indifference to the verities of religion, but we do not live under the mastery and sway of the will of Almighty God. Were I to take the time, I think I could prove to my own satisfaction that our history here in America clearly reveals that our national life from the beginning until now has been feeble or strong according as the faith of our people has been feeble or strong. Our most prosperous and peaceful periods have been when we honored and believed in the Bible and supported the church and tried to live our faith out in obedience to God. If we lose eventually, if we give up our overmastering consciousness of God, if we desert spiritual religion, then we must forfeit our hope of a nation in which human aspirations can be disciplined and brought to fulfillment.

If you forget everything else I have said in this message, remember this one sentence; without our fathers' faith we cannot build a world like our fathers did before us. The revitalization of our ideals, the restoration of our conscience, the revival of our spiritual faith—these are the three essentials.

A great soldier, General Omar Bradley, said the other day: "We have too many men of science, too few men of God. We have grasped the mystery of the atom, and rejected the Sermon on the Mount. The world has achieved brilliance without wisdom, power without conscience. Ours is a world of nuclear giants and ethical infants. We know more about war than we know about peace, more about killing than we know about living."

John Foster Dulles, the great Secretary of State and fine Christian layman, just before his untimely death said: "What we lack is a righteous and dynamic faith, for without it all else avails us little. This lack cannot be compensated for by politicians, however able, or by diplomats, however astute, or by scientists, however inventive, or by bombs, however powerful." We must have a righteous and dynamic faith.

In succeeding messages, I shall be dwelling further with equal earnestness upon this matter of a revival of spiritual religion, a restoration of these great convictions, the starting again of these hidden currents of faith, idealism, and prayer.

Making a Faith of Our Own

"Jesus of Nazareth is passing by."

—*Luke 18:37*

The scriptural springboard for this message, chosen from the
lesson found in Luke 18:35-43, is the simple statement, "They told
him, 'Jesus of Nazareth is passing by.'" It takes me back to a
Sunday-school song of my boyhood days.

> Jesus is passing by,
> Jesus is passing by;
> Bring Him thy heart
> ere in grief He depart;
> Jesus is passing by.

It is my clear and compelling conviction that a man insults his
intelligence, impoverishes his life, and puts his soul in jeopardy
unless and until he thinks his way to some great and overmastering
convictions concerning the Lord Jesus Christ. If we understood
oriental conditions and people as they lived and labored at the
time of Christ, if we knew them a little better, fresh significance
and light would break forth from many of the pages of the New
Testament. This story is an illustration.

Jesus was making his way toward Jericho. Then as now the roads

32

were lined with the blind, the lame, the deaf, the diseased, and the unfortunate of every sort. In this company of unfortunates was the man who but for Jesus is the chief character in the story. With the instinct that so often accompanies blindness, he sensed that some extraordinary event was happening, that some unusual person was passing by and he cried out: "What is all this about? Who is passing by?"

"Jesus of Nazareth is passing by," replied those nearby, seeking to quiet him.

Staggering to his feet, he pressed out into the road and with great earnestness begged for his sight.

Then Jesus said to him, "Receive your sight; your faith has made you well."

"Immediately he received his sight and followed him, glorifying God; and all the people, when they saw it, gave praise to God." That is the scriptural story. I repeat, if we knew more of oriental conditions and life in Palestine at that time, new light would break out from every line in this story.

"Jesus of Nazareth is passing by." I suppose life will run out for me before I understand some very good friends of mine—lovely people, cultured people, well-intentioned people committed to decency, but people who have never thought their way through to any great and overwhelming beliefs concerning Christ. How people, if they are mentally awake, can live in a world in which Christ has played such a part and over which he has had such marvelous influence and not have conceived some deep convictions concerning him, I do not know.

These friends of mine remind me of the Roman soldiers who, under orders, took Jesus out to put him to death. When they had nailed him to the cross, lifted it, and dropped it in its place, they immediately fell on their knees and on the back of a shield started gambling for his clothing. So far as the record goes, they never looked up at him again. They were finished with him. Their own pleasures, the pursuit of their own desires monopolized them. There he was, just above their heads, the unique and the solitary Son of God. There he was, the Savior of the world. There he was, the Judge of men and nations. There he was, the world's hope for time and eternity; but so far as we know, they never looked up. They were too busy gambling for his clothing. They sought only something for themselves. There are people all around us, who never know Christ. He passes by, but they never look up.

Then there are a few people who move a little from this state of utter indifference. They admit that Jesus was a majestic figure upon the pages of history. They give him an unusual place and buy post cards showing him with a halo about his head. When they use his name on certain occasions, they lower their voice and refer to him with dreamy affection in a soothing manner. I am not ridiculing that attitude. Nevertheless, I am reminded that it was Renan who called Jesus that "sweet Galilean," but it took an old Scottish preacher named Chalmers, who did not like that approach, to say, "Let us be done with all of these nursery endearments."

In support of my opening statement, I repeat that we insult our intelligence, we impoverish our lives, we put our souls in jeopardy, we miss life's fairest and finest until, like this blind man, we begin to inquire about him and to think our way into great convictions concerning him. Mirrored in this story is the whole gospel story. This blind man stands for the plight of man, and Christ is here with his power.

I would share with you some of the basic facts about Jesus Christ, fully attested by history, which reveal the major sentiments of my mind and soul. Would that we might all arrive at these mastering conclusions which lead us to surrender our wills to his life and purpose. Let me point the way.

First, *we must give him our undivided attention and complete loyalty, because Jesus Christ is the central figure upon all the pages of history.* Some years ago a London publication employed H. G. Wells to prepare a list of the twelve greatest characters to be found anywhere upon the vast stage of history. Mr. Wells was the great philosopher, the great historian of his day, but he was not a Christian as we measure Christians. He did not bring to his task religious devotion and worship as you or I would bring. He was a cold, calculating historian. He turned the pages of history, all of them, and reviewed the whole procession of humanity's great parading down the corridors of time—kings, emperors, heroes, sages, the mighty of the ages. When Mr. Wells concluded his study, Jesus of Nazareth was the name that headed his list. He could not avoid the choice. He could not be an honest historian and not put him first.

No man can write an authentic history of the human race and not put Jesus Christ first. But granting that his name is above every name does not alone make one a Christian. It simply makes one an honest student of human history. In all this procession of humanity out of all the centuries, across all the continents, Jesus Christ of Nazareth is the central figure. All history prior to his cross converges at his cross, and all subsequent history diverges from his cross. James A. Francis pays this tribute to him:

Here is a man who was born in an obscure village, the child of a peasant woman. He grew up in an obscure village. He worked in a carpenter shop until he was thirty, and then for three years he was an itinerant preacher. He never wrote a book. He never held an office. He never owned a home. He never had a family. He never went to college. He never traveled two hundred miles from the place where he was born.

He never did one of the things that usually accompany greatness. He had no credentials but himself. . . . While still a young man, the tide of popular opinion turned against him. His friends ran away. One of them denied him. He was turned over to his enemies. He went through the mockery of a trial. He was nailed to a cross between two thieves. His executioners gambled for the only piece of property he had on earth while he was dying—his coat. When he was dead he was taken down and laid in a borrowed grave through the pity of a friend.

Nineteen wide centuries have come and gone; today he is the center-piece of the human race and the Leader of the column of progress.

I am far within the mark when I say that all the armies that ever marched, and all the navies that ever were built, and all the parliaments that ever sat, and all the kings that ever reigned, put together, have not affected the life of man upon this earth as powerfully as has this *one solitary life.*

Religion need not be a factor in this appraisal of Jesus of Nazareth. One need only be a fair-minded person, an accurate student of history to discover that he is the central figure of all human history. Who else could divide history into two parts—before and after his coming? When Pilate washed his cowardly hands before the mob and said, "I am innocent of this man's blood; see to it yourselves," I suppose he thought that he was washing Jesus off the pages of history, that nobody would remember him in a few years. Significantly enough, in less than a hundred years nobody remembered Pilate except as he appeared in the presence of Jesus. Pilate has dropped into oblivion, but the name of Jesus is as precious and as powerful today as it has ever been since the day his enemies sent him to the cross. More books have been written about him in the last hundred years than in any hundred years since his death. Those of us who acknowledge Jesus as Lord are worshiping him who is undeniably the central figure in all human history.

Other men have been accounted great. Among them have been those whose names have struck terror to the hearts of decent people. There have been times in history when these tyrants would move, and good men and women everywhere would tremble lest they come their way. Now those mighty ones are all gone.

Recently I was in Vienna, one of the loveliest European cities. It used to be the gayest city in Europe. Today it tries to laugh, but ends in tears because its empire is gone. During the years that I was in Austria, I always stayed at the Ambassador Hotel in Vienna. It is a delightful place to stay. A plaque on one side of the lobby said that Theodore Roosevelt slept there and one on the opposite side that Mark Twain slept there. Although I have slept there a good many times, no plaque commemorates my presence, but for some unknown reason I was always given room 510. A special attraction to me, in addition to its comfort, was its location across the street from one of the famous monasteries of the world, the Monastery and Church of the Capuchins.

In the basement of that monastery Austria has buried her distinguished sons and daughters for centuries. In other years I have spent many hours down there. The other day I went again with my party and then I went back alone, just to wander around the place. One hundred and forty-four caskets rest on the floor, one less than formerly. Napoleon's only son slept there in his ornate casket for over a century, but when Hitler took Vienna, he sent that casket to Paris to repose under the same roof with Napoleon's. The next time you go to Paris, look around when you visit Napoleon's tomb and you will see the son's casket not far from the father's.

There in Vienna in the Capuchin Monastery are buried kings and queens, princes and princesses, dukes and generals, the great of empire—144 of them. The magnificence of some of their caskets begs description. Maria Theresa is entombed there with all her many children around her. Yonder is the casket of Archduke Ferdinand, whose assassination touched off World War I, which has never completely ended. Here lie in death the once so-called great of earth. These were the tyrants. These were the people who held the world in awe. They had their little day, but dropped into oblivion. Now they are almost forgotten.

On the fateful day of the border closing, which marked the beginning of the present-continuing crisis, I arrived once again in Berlin. When my episcopal assignment was Europe, I spent much time there. My duties in Poland to the east, Czechoslovakia to the south, and Belgium to the west made it the natural place of residence, and I came to love the city. It was full of excitement for von Hindenburg was losing out and Hitler was coming into power. Standing in the rain with young Germans before Hitler's Chancellery, I heard them shout, "Heil Hitler! Heil Hitler!" until their emotions lifted to such a frenzied pitch as I had never before witnessed. Once Hitler came out on the balcony and made a speech. Although I did not understand German, I am sure he told them he was going to build a Germany that would last forever.

On this most recent visit, I went over into East Berlin because much of the Berlin that I once had known is still in that sector controlled by the Soviets. I stood on the site of the Chancellery where Hitler had lived and found myself gazing into sheer space. Grass was struggling to grow on the leveled ground. Every trace of the imposing structure was gone.

"Where is this man," I asked, "who was going to build a Germany that would last forever?"

"He died a suicide," was the reply, "with a bad woman at his side, and a German sergeant poured enough gasoline on them to turn them to a cinder so that there were even no ashes."

Hitler is gone, but the church he was trying to destroy is having something like a revival in Germany, even in East Germany where Communism is doing its best to stamp out religion. My friend, the Bishop of East Germany, preaches to great crowds. Tyrants come and we tremble. We think that they are going to wreck the world. They come and they go, but Jesus of Nazareth remains. His is the name that endures. Kingdoms rise and fall, but he goes on forever —the central figure in all human history.

Simply to be mentally awake, aside from all spiritual interests, and to leave Jesus out of your thinking and out of your living is to insult your intelligence, to impoverish your life, to put your soul in jeopardy. If someone were to find a long-lost scroll in the sands of Egypt and prove the authenticity of a command therein contained that once had fallen from his lips and then somehow was lost; although they had never heard of it before, millions of people in the world would try to obey it or die attempting to do so. He is not on his way out. He is the central figure of our world. When memory loses all other names, when all else is in ruins, when the great names of history are forgotten, the name of Jesus will flame forth in undiminished glory.

Second, *his life and his teaching have become the foundation upon which we have built all that is good and best in our civilization.* History teaches the careful student that nations which would have none of him, which rejected him, have faded into nothingness. They had their little day, but their bright morning ended in night and they have gone the way of dust. The reverse is also true. The nations that have even partially accepted him, that have partially obeyed his teaching, that have followed in some measure what he said about God and life and duty and justice and brotherhood—these are the nations that have been able to build all that is fine and good and enduring and uplifting in our civilization. Go anywhere in the world and look for the best form of democracy; look for the best

39

schools; try to ascertain who has the best government; see where working people have the greatest privileges and the largest place in civilization. Wherever he has been accepted and is beloved and followed, nations have come to their fullest flower.

Years ago I read a story of a man who bought his seven-year-old daughter a model village, a miniature town with homes and churches and hospitals and government buildings. He set it up in the home, and she greatly admired it.

Seeking to teach her a lesson, he suggested one day, "Let's take out everything that is here as a result of the teachings of Jesus." He took out the church. Then he took out the schools, for Christianity is the mother of education. Next he took out the hospitals. One by one he removed the institutions that have their origin in what Jesus said about God or life or man.

Soon the little girl broke into tears and said to her father, "Daddy, nobody would want to live in a town like that." How true. We accept so many of these components that give us life and civilization and order and health without inquiring into their source. We are like the farmer who takes the recurring seasons for granted and fails to see the God who is back of them.

In the Congo some years ago a Christian chief invited a cynical American, who was not a Christian, to dine with him. During the simple meal the American guest saw a Bible on a nearby table and, trying to be funny, uttered some blasphemous words about it. The old chief held up his hand in protest and said, "Don't say that, don't say that. But for that Book I would be eating you now rather than eating with you."

And so it is. We enjoy a civilization where life is good and civilization is strong and hope is firm. When we trace it back to its origin, we discover that Jesus of Nazareth really made it so. Upon his teaching, the best we know in civilization is built and based.

Nobody would want to live in a world where his teachings had been utterly rejected. From him we have gathered inspiration, not for good living alone, but also for the noblest and most unselfish service —so much so that the very terms Christianity and civilization are almost synonymous. Jesus has not only given us the hope of heaven, but he has touched everything in the earth around about us. *He has sanctified the whole round of life.* Life day by day is sweeter and better because he enabled it.

Take labor. There was a time when men thought labor was a curse sent from God because of man's sin. One day Jesus stood in a carpenter shop in Nazareth and pushed a plane with his own hand, working as a laboring man. Then suddenly man discovered that labor was not a curse but a noble task. The distance between the communion table and a man's worktable is not great. One can labor, whether it be practicing law, rearing children, or running a farm, with such consecrated motives that day by day he glorifies God. Work and worship are closely allied. The work that was once thought of as a curse has been ennobled and made glorious because he engaged in it.

Take childhood. There was a time when nobody loved children. They had no value placed upon them until they were old enough to earn something. Then Jesus came into the world as a baby and slept in his mother's arms, thereby sanctifying the children of the world. The most miserly of men will usually give something to children. Jesus set the babies of the world in the center of our affection. They never would have been there but for him and what he said about childhood.

Take womanhood. Woman was without honor and dignity. She was not considered to be a person. Even today she has no dignity or privilege or influence except where the teaching of Jesus has been accepted. In the Congo men once bought their wives with copper crosses. The dowry they were compelled to give to get the bride was most important, and if the husband died, she would revert to the father as would a piece of land. Woman was just a chattel, a piece of property without rights or dignity. Woman's plight was sorry indeed until Jesus was born of a woman, slept in a woman's arms, and said to John from the cross, "Behold thy mother." Those baby hands, those pierced hands of his lifted women up until every Christian man likes to take off his hat and make his bow in the presence of a good woman.

Take the cross. It was once the symbol of everything that was ugly and heinous in human life. Because it was so odious, his enemies nailed him to it; they sought to disgrace him forever. Instead of remaining the ugly, repugnant, hated object it once was, the cross became the symbol of all that is precious in your life and mine. The grave once evoked the greatest dread imaginable, but when he slept in a grave and arose from it to declare, "I am alive for evermore," even death was transformed from an end to a beginning, from a sunset to a sunrise.

Jesus of Nazareth is our hope for time and eternity. If our world is to have hope, if it is to face the future unafraid, if it is to have sanity, if it is to have security, if it is to have satisfaction, if it is to have salvation, it all must come from him. There is no sanity for our social order, there is no satisfaction for these restless spirits of ours except in him. He is our hope in this life as well as in the life to come. Not our strivings, not our good works, not our deeds of charity but Christ doing for us that which we cannot do for ourselves is the key to the abundant life.

Let me share with you this wonderful statement:

The critics may come with their spectacles and their scissors and their paste and take apart His gospel, tear it to pieces. But when they have finished, the voice of Jesus still speaks and the eyes of Jesus still look into our souls. Time and time again men have declared that He was out of date and that He ought to be buried. Some have attacked Him scornfully with bitter anger in their eyes. Some have forsaken Him sadly with lingering regret. But somehow, He always appears as the judge of His judges. An age of luxury may reject His discipline, but time will make it clear that it was wrong. An age of materialism may reject His idealism, but our children will come seeking Him again. An age of scientific knowledge may spurn His simplicity, but men will come back again and again with outstretched arms and empty hearts to ask Him the deep unanswered questions of the human soul. He is our hope in this life.

Whoever the man may be, however far astray he may have wandered, however low down in sin he may have fallen, God can restore him. Christ will lift him up out of the mire of sin into decency and respectability, into strength and joy. As long as Jesus of Nazareth is near, we need not faint; as long as his love is ours, we need not falter.

Life Takes On New Meaning

"I gave you a land on which you had not labored. . . .
"Now therefore fear the Lord, and serve him in sincerity and in
faithfulness."

—*Josh. 24:13-14*

The significant words of the text chosen for this message were
spoken by a remarkable man on a most extraordinary occasion.
The human race has produced few greater characters than Joshua.
The swift passing of the centuries has witnessed few greater occasions than the mighty assembly of the people of Israel to whom these
words were first spoken. Joshua had been the leader of the people
of God for a long time and under his leadership and wisdom prosperity and expansion had come to the people. He was now an old
man and must soon relinquish his place to another. As old age came
upon this venerable leader, a fearful crisis developed in the life of
the nation. Instead of walking in faithful obedience before Jehovah,
the people were turning aside to strange gods. As a result of this
national apostasy, Joshua called them together in a great assembly
and delivered to them one of the most remarkable addresses you
can find in any literature. If you would like to read a great speech,
you need not consult a copy of the *Congressional Record;* just read
the address of Joshua when he spoke to his beloved nation in a time
of crisis and confusion. We will not review that speech in its en-

tirety; but he reminded them of the period when they were a horde of slaves in Egypt. He talked to them of their original and inexpressible debt to Almighty God for the miraculous deliverance at the Red Sea. He told them of God's kindly providences and discipline as they wandered for years in the wilderness.

He came to the climax of this great address when, speaking for the Lord, he said to his ungrateful people: " 'I gave you a land on which you had not labored, and cities which you had not built, and you dwell therein; you eat the fruit of vineyards and oliveyards which you did not plant.'

"Now therefore fear the Lord, and serve him in sincerity and in faithfulness."

Whatever the faults of America, we cannot forget the Christian faith which made this great country. It is good that across the vast stretches of this land of ours multitudes of people, out of the busy life and bigness of our nation, gather in churches to acknowledge their debt to Almighty God. Thanksgiving Day, at its best, should awaken in us a fresh sense of our debt to the Father and of our dependence upon him. It should create in us the responsiveness which acknowledges not only the abundance of his gifts, but that he is the source and sustainer of life. A service on this national holiday should fasten our attention not only upon our gifts but upon the Giver.

When we contemplate God's providential leadership, his forgiving mercy, his sustaining grace, his kindly disciplines, we are moved to say with the Psalmist:

> Bless the Lord, O my soul,
>   and forget not all his benefits.

No offering we can make on this day will be quite so appropriate as the offering of a thankful heart. Thanksgiving is not only a duty but a delight; an awakened heart and mind mean inevitably a thankful heart.

Let us acknowledge at the outset that all we have, all we know, all we enjoy has come to us not as the reward of our own striving, not as a result of our labors, not because we have gone into the fields and caught up the raw materials and fashioned something for ourselves. We live, in fact, in a land for which we have not labored; we dwell in cities of refuge, of blessing, and of privilege which we have not built. We eat the fruit that sustains us in a thousand ways, from vineyards whose planting we did not attend. All has come to us out of the tears and toils, out of the faith and fidelity, out of the slow and painful striving of those who came before us, who lived in the fear of Almighty God and bequeathed to us the civilization that is ours.

A simple and practical illustration is *our American homelife.* If ever a people enjoyed a rich and privileged homelife, it is the people of America. The sun has never looked down upon any group of people quite so blessed, quite so fortunate, quite so unburdened as you and I in the security, the abundance, and the guardianship of our Christian home. If there is a basic institution in our civilization, it is the Christian home. If one wants to know what kind of nation we shall have fifty years hence, see what is happening in the homes, the schools, and the churches today. The nation of tomorrow is being fashioned now by our faith, our fidelity, our convictions about God and duty, life, and destiny; and by what we believe and teach children in our homes today.

Years ago I had a friend who was prominent in the Y.M.C.A. He and his wife traveled around the world for nearly a year in a day when going around the world was quite an achievement. They landed, at the end of their journey, in San Francisco and walked to their hotel. The wife missed the husband for a moment and turned to see that he had stopped to pick up a small, unkempt stray dog and was carrying him as he quickened his steps to catch up with her.

In response to her questioning glance he said: "I am reminding myself that the plain people here in America have a better chance at life and liberty than the common people have in many of the nations in which we have been traveling and that even a dumb animal like this is able to find a good home and a compassionate master."

If there is a basic institution in our civilization, it is the Christian home. If my objective were to destroy America, root and branch, this is the place I would first attack. Out of the Christian home have come the good things that comprise our way of life. Before God ever ordained a minister, before ever there was a lovely sanctuary, Paul, in sending greetings to friends, wrote, "Greet also the church in their house."

The whole idea of government comes from the authority of the parents over growing children. The first hospital had its inception when some kind-hearted, tender-handed mother took soft cloths and, with home remedies, ministered to the hurt of her children. The first school was founded when some truth-loving, sincere parents taught the growing minds of their children the basic principles of life. All the great and essential institutions which, put together, make up Christian civilization had their birth in the Christian home. We do not need to look elsewhere to discover that we live in a land for which we did not labor and eat the fruit of vineyards we did not plant. Practically all this security was wrought out by the faith and fidelity of our forefathers.

In the Congress, Daniel Webster made a great speech in which he spoke of the home of his childhood:

My father and my mother built their first little cabin home upon the bleak hills of New Hampshire. There I was born, there I grew and there

47

they trained me. The years have gone by, the cabin is down and there stands only the ruin of the chimney to mark its location, but once a year I go back to that spot and stand beside that chimney, with my head uncovered, to remind myself of their sacrifice and of their self-forgetfulness. [Then the great statesman and orator added what is perhaps his greatest statement], If ever I forget that what I am is the result of what they did for me, who they were, God grant that my name may be blotted forever out of the book and out of the memory of mankind.

I remind you and your children that our homelife which is so precious, so secure, and so abundant is not the product of our striving. It is not something we bought and paid for, but something bequeathed to us by men and women of fidelity, who wrought it out for us in toil and pain.

All that we enjoy today *of national life,* of power and prestige, has likewise come to us out of the vision and work of men and women who have passed from this earthly scene. This is not the Fourth of July, not a flag-waving time, but a time to meditate upon a nation—our nation—founded by faith. One need not be a religious fanatic to find the handwriting of Almighty God over all the walls of this republic.

The New World was discovered by Columbus in 1492, but nearly 140 years passed before there was any real effort to colonize and develop this continent. If the Spanish had come from Florida and conquered it or if the French had come down from Canada and developed it, our government would have been a monarchy, and the dominant religion would inevitably have been Roman Catholic. Does not God seem to have deterred these great powers? In Europe, especially in Northern Europe, during these 140 years, there was a great revival of evangelical religion, a revival that opened the Bible for every man to read, and as men read they discovered they were not born slaves but freemen, the children of God, endowed with inalienable rights. They banded themselves together into cramped, worm-eaten ships and crossed the wide Atlantic. Their purpose was not to build just another nation, but one that was righteous and ministering. Before the Mayflower had touched shore, after having been driven five hundred miles off its course by contrary winds, they fell to their knees in thanksgiving and wrote down for the pages of history, "We are building this nation for the glory of God and the spread of the Christian religion." They were not here for conquest; they were not motivated by selfishness. Those Pilgrims had to pay twenty-three years for their passage. One hundred and two of them came and fifty-four died that first year. They did not put mounds over the graves, but leveled and covered them with leaves so that the hostile Indians would not see how fast they were diminishing. All of this was for the glory of God and the spread of the Christian religion.

Sometime ago I was in an American city where, in the afternoon, I was to preach a great mass meeting. I did not attend church that morning, but turned on the radio in my hotel room to listen to a Thanksgiving sermon. The minister said three things about our Pilgrim fathers, three things so pertinent that I wished I might have been the one to think of them. I am like the Indian who, knowing nothing of communication other than smoke signaling, saw the atomic bomb erupt over New Mexico and said, "My, I wish I had thought of that!" These are the brief words the minister said about our founding fathers, "They left, they came, they stayed." Here in a nutshell is much of our American history. They left bondage and tyranny. They came through mountainous seas on a strange and unknown path and, once they were here, they dedicated their act with devotion. They endured that first winter without sufficient food, being at one time reduced to five grains of parched corn per person, and when the abundance of harvest had returned, Thanksgiving Day was inaugurated. On that day before they placed the turkey, the cranberry sauce, and the other rich trimmings upon the tables, they put five grains of corn upon the upturned plates of their children to remind them that this abundance, these ideals, convictions, and privileges had come, not with ease, but through starvation nigh unto death.

You and I live in a land for which we have labored very little; we eat the fruit of vineyards we did not plant; we live in cities of learning that others have built for us where we enjoy unfettered consciences and exalted privileges. *All that we have of Christian hope and doctrine was secured to us* by the faith and fidelity, by the unswerving allegiance, and sometimes by the death of men who gave their lives to preserve these verities. There is hardly a man among us who does not believe in the Resurrection. He may not come to church, but he believes that somewhere, somehow, he will make his peace with God and greet his loved ones on the other side. This hope of life after death undergirds our everyday living. If this belief of life everlasting were taken from our world, our homes would become places of mourning and our world would wrap itself in a mantle of despair. The most unworthy man gets some sustenance, some strength from believing that death is not an end. This doctrine of immortality sustains all of us, but from whence did it come? You may answer, "The Lord gave it to us." True, but God has never been able to give us any great liberating truth until he could find some man bigger than his day, who could see beyond his own self-interest and his own little group and live in terms of subsequent centuries.

Paul was a very likable preacher; he was a great scholar and perfectly at home among the learned of his day. He brooked no opposition until he preached the one comprehensive truth that Jesus Christ was the Son of God, that Joseph's grave could not hold him, that on the third day he arose and by his resurrection guaranteed everlasting life to his followers. That was the gospel that Paul preached and with it came trouble—hate, imprisonment, and eventually death. All this for no reason other than that he preached what today we believe, namely, that there is life after death, that Jesus Christ broke the bonds of death, shattered the tyranny of the grave, and that death is not an ending but a beginning. Paul was respected in the synagogue until he preached this truth and then he was arrested and put into prison.

There is a story or legend to the effect that the Roman emperor sent a messenger to Paul in prison, saying in effect, "Paul, we have nothing against you except that you go on preaching this nonsense about the Resurrection. If you will promise to give it up and go on back home to your tentmaking and be done with this troublesome idea, we will let you live; we will not put you to death."

The legend, true or false as it may be, tells us that Paul turned his face to the messenger and said, "Go tell the emperor that so long as this tongue of mine is not dust I shall proclaim the evangel of God."

Strike! The blade fell! The head went into the basket! I tremble to imagine where you and I would be if Paul had chosen to save his own life. I tremble to think what kind of Christianity we would have in our world if he had put his comforts above his cause. He forgot himself into immortality and, by dying for this truth of life after death, turned it loose on the world and gave it wings. Our hope for time and eternity rests upon that broken sepulcher. Our living Lord was secured to us not only by the goodness of God but also by the unwearied suffering of a man who thought in terms of the future.

Take that great *doctrine,* which we call *justification by faith.* We all believe in it, and let us thank God for it. It tells us that a man can be saved by a simple act of penitence and faith in the Lord Jesus Christ. This doctrine has not always been in the world. God is always trying to give us great truths, but he cannot until someone forgets himself into immortality. Every great truth in this whole body of Christian doctrine was brought to us upon the stooped shoulders and over the bleeding feet of men who forgot themselves. For this liberating truth, justification by faith, someone had to suffer.

Martin Luther was a respected priest in the Roman Catholic church. A scholar of great intellectual attainments and courage, he possessed every gift that makes a man a conspicuous leader. He was in Rome climbing up the so-called "sacred stairs." I saw them not long ago and bristled with indignation while viewing them. There I saw men and women down on their knees, repeating a *Pater Noster* for each step and kissing the step in the hope of delivering some soul from purgatory. Four centuries ago, Martin Luther was down on his knees climbing these stairs, believing that the way to get to God was to suffer, to endure penance, to wear a shirt of hair, or to climb on bleeding knees up these "sacred stairs." When he reached the top, legend has it that Luther raised himself and exclaimed, "The just shall live by faith."

Luther arose, wiped the blood from his knees, and went back to his church to write ninety-five theses which he nailed on the church door. They declared that the way out of sin and to God is not up some sacred stairs, but over an old-fashioned hill called Calvary.

You know what happened. This young preacher was summoned to court where the authorities of church and state frowned upon him. When he came forward to meet his accusers, the good women of the parish ran to him and said, "Brother Luther, you will never come again; you must not go."

"I must go," he replied. "If the devils are as thick as the tiles on the housetops, I must go"

As he went in for his trial, a German soldier saluted him and said, "God have mercy upon your soul, you poor, helpless monk."

The authorities faced Luther, saying, "We demand you retract this nonsense."

"This is God's truth," Luther replied. "I have announced it; I can do no other." As they rose to do him harm, God stayed their hand, and Luther separated from them, a free man.

I can go to the humblest little chapel in the hills and tell sinning humanity that they do not have to go to Rome, they do not have to climb steps, they do not have to wear shirts of hair, they do not have to perform acts of penance. All they have to do is to say, "God, be merciful to me, a sinner. I come in the name of Christ."

Then and there salvation comes to them. All that we know and all that we enjoy of saving truth that undergirds and sustains life has come out of the goodness of God, but these truths have been defended, preserved, and passed on to us by men and women who could live beyond their own little day.

This blessed *truth of universal salvation* that has not always been in our world is available for all men. I am aware of the fact that the wind bloweth where it listeth, and when God wants to send truth into the world, he does not have to take some particular channel to do it. John and Charles Wesley were very orthodox men, exact in their ritualism, bound by their sacramental interpretation of the Scriptures, thinking that salvation was for a few people and that some of the sins of some people could be forgiven. This approach, however, did not satisfy their hungry hearts or the hearts of the people. Someone observed that it was as if they were seated at the table of the church of their day and found little to eat. They began to examine the table and found it was an extension table. John grasped one end and Charles the other and they extended it until it encircled the globe. Then John ran to the front door and Charles to the back, each ringing a dinner bell and shouting, "O come all ye that are athirst." Salvation is not for a few people on a few occasions; it is for all men for all time. The universality of the gospel took wings. All we have, all we know, all we enjoy has come from the liberal hands of the Great Giver himself, but truth has been defended and spread abroad in the world by people with a passion for unselfishness.

With earnestness and almost a fierceness of conviction, I say that these great gifts given to us by Almighty God are under furious assault at this moment. One does not have to be a pessimist to know that the battle is joined. Forces are loose in the world that would steal away these gifts, that would rob our children of these indispensable ideals. Forces are at work in America that would openly attack the Christian home, that would destroy the whole idea of a monogamous family. Forces are active here in our beloved land that would emasculate the life of our churches and make of them a kind of comfortable country club. Forces backed by powerful armies are turned loose in the world, willing to sacrifice for their propaganda which, if successful, would keep America from being any longer a land of evangelical religion.

Abraham Lincoln said in one of his thanksgiving-day proclamations:

It is the duty of nations, as well as men, to own their dependence upon the overruling power of God, to confess their sins and transgressions in humble sorrow, yet with the sure hope that genuine repentance will lead to mercy and pardon, and to recognize the sublime truth announced in the Holy Scriptures, and proven by all history, that nations are blessed only when God is their Lord. We have been the recipients of the choicest bounties of heaven, we have been preserved these many years in peace and prosperity, we have grown, but we have forgotten too often the gracious hand which preserved us in peace, and multiplied, enriched and strengthened us, and we have vainly imagined, in the deceitfulness of our hearts, that all these blessings were produced by some superior wisdom and virtue of our own. Intoxicated with unbroken success, we have become too self-sufficient to feel the necessity of redeeming and preserving grace, and too proud to pray to the God who made us. It behooves us to humble ourselves before the offended power, to confess our national sins, and to ask God for his forgiveness.

This is what I must say to America this day. This mania for materialism, this magic of things, this upside down sense of values blinds us to the fact that our peace, our prosperity, our power, our liberty, our learning, yea, all the things that comprise our American Christian way of life are again under attack. We must love these ideals, defend, and promote them so that our children can some day say, "We live in a land for which we did not labor; it was out of the faith and fidelity of our fathers that these liberties came to us."

In the Old Testament there is the lovely story of David who, while leading his armies in battle, drew near his boyhood home in the little town of Bethlehem. One night, weary with war and the responsibilities of leadership, David said longingly, "O that someone would give me water to drink from the well of Bethlehem which is by the gate!" He thirsted for water from the old well where he used to drink when he was a boy. I do not know how much of David's thirst was actually for water, but I do know that when life gets hard and the burdens heavy, when the duties are many and tasks formidable, we long to cast aside our troubles and go back to the scenes of our childhood. Memory has a way of making the past seem better than it really was. We can go on a picnic, get drenched by rain, and find ants devouring our lunch, but when we tell the story in after years, we forget the ants and the rain and remember the picnic as a happy occasion. God made us this way; our memories sort out the unfortunate and disagreeable experiences and cast them aside. If we remembered all of our tragedies, we would break from the heavy load they put upon us. But life is not as good as we imagine it to be; the good we magnify and the poor we forget.

So David longed for his youth; he was tired of being a general. The Philistines occupied Bethlehem, and he must do combat with them. It was then that he cried out for a drink from the well of Bethlehem. Three of his chief soldiers, "three mighty men," resolved to fetch it. They crawled out into No Man's Land, "broke through the camp of the Philistines," and at last dipped their vessel into the cool refreshing waters of the well beside the gate of Bethlehem. They fought their way back until they came into the presence of David and handed him that which he so desired. He took the vessel, looked at the water within it, looked long at the men who had brought it, and then slowly "he poured it out to the Lord," saying, "Far be it from me, O Lord, that I should do this. Shall I drink the blood of the men who went at the risk of their lives?" He could not use for his personal gratification that which cost his men so much. When he saw how they had suffered and put their lives in jeopardy to secure the water, it was too holy to be used in satisfying his own thirst.

This inheritance out of the gracious hands of God, watered by the tears and baptized in the blood of God-fearing, liberty-loving men and women, is too great for us to squander or let perish. We dare not take this heritage without accepting the responsibility for its preservation. We cannot live in a land which we did not build and not hear these other words, "Now therefore fear the Lord, and serve him in sincerity and in faithfulness."

In Schuylerville, New York, a great monument stands in the public square, a memorial designed to honor four generals of the Revolutionary War. On one of its four sides is a statue of General Washington and on two of the remaining three sides are statues of General Schuyler and General Gates, all great defenders of our nation.

If you walk around to the fourth side, you will see a niche in which another figure was to be placed, but it is empty. An old resident will tell you that when this monument was originally conceived, it was to honor Washington, Schuyler, Gates, and Arnold but before the war was over, Benedict Arnold had proved himself a traitor. That is why one niche was left vacant. It is an everlasting reminder of a man who failed his country in a crucial hour.

We cannot accept our gifts simply to enjoy them; we cannot go into our houses of plenty, eat from our tables laden with abundance simply to use them for our own gratification, merely to satiate our own selfish appetites. If we should do so, there would forever be a vacant niche testifying to the fact that we took and never gave, that we enjoyed but left others poorer after we had been satisfied. We cannot pay our debt to the past until we have put the future in debt to us.

The Tenderness of God's Love

"See what love the Father has given us."

—1 John 3:1

Over in one of his letters John tells us about the redeeming love of God. "See what the Father has given us, that we should be called children of God; and so we are. . . . Beloved, we are God's children now; it does not yet appear what we shall be, but we know that when he appears we shall be like him, for we shall see him as he is. And every one who thus hopes in him purifies himself as he is pure." (I John 3:1-3.)

As the years of my life lengthen, I find it more and more difficult to attempt a sermon concerning the love of God. Not that I do not believe in it; I never believed in it so profoundly as I do now. As life is prolonged, my trust in the measureless love of God grows and deepens and widens until I find it difficult to find words which adequately express what I think of his boundless devotion to his children. As we gaze up toward his divine heights or as we look out on his limitless expanses, words become such a feeble mode of expression. We cannot sound the depth of his love, we cannot soar to its heights, we cannot measure its circumference. It dwarfs all of our standards. It tosses aside all our metaphors and runs ahead of all our human comparisons. It is deeper than all the seas. It is higher than all the heavens. It is brighter than all the suns. It is more enduring than all the ages. It is stronger than sin. It is deeper than sorrow. It is mightier than death. Fire cannot consume it. Hate cannot baffle it. Darkness cannot obscure it. No wonder Frederick W. Faber wrote:

> For the love of God is broader
> Than the measures of a man's mind,
> And the heart of the Eternal
> Is most wonderfully kind.

"See what love the Father has given us, that we should be called children of God."

The value of any religion is determined by the revelation of God which it brings and the possibility of communion with God which it offers. What it says to us about God and the opportunity it offers us to come again into the favor and the family of God are basic. Certain key words bring us to some appreciation of this entire text. Down through the long ages, men have marveled at the extent and the patience of the love of God. Perhaps no man ever lived who knew more of the love of God or who walked in more blessed intimacy with God than did the author of this text. Out of his knowledge and his intimate fellowship with God he has written for you and me, "See what love the Father has given us," or as the King James translation has it, "Behold, what manner of love the Father hath bestowed upon us."

Let us study the first word, "see" or "behold." Years ago I noticed that chapter after chapter of the Word of God has for its first word, "behold." I asked myself if there was some special message in the word. I wondered if, apart from what followed it, there was some special significance to that particular beginning. I concluded that there is. Traveling on the public highways, you have noticed at railroad crossings a sign in the shape of a cross warning, "Stop, look, and listen." If you were giving heed, that silent post commanded your attention. It demanded the concentration of every power you possessed on what was then at hand. It summoned you to withdraw your attention from everything else and fasten it on the immediate situation. This word "behold" has that kind of significance. It commands attention. It demands thought. It insists that all else be pushed aside and forgotten for the moment and that we stand reverently and responsively in the presence of the love of God.

In addition it carries the idea of exclamation, of wonder, of awe, of surprise. Motoring with my family some years ago through the Rockies, I remember as the car would swing around the bend of some mountain road and a majestic mountain would lift its head or a lovely mountain valley would unfold before us, everyone in the car would exclaim at the same moment, "Look!" That was about all we could say. None of us could describe the majesty of the mountain. None of us could depict the loveliness of the valley, and so we threw up our mental hands, as it were, in adoration and wonder, crying, "Look!" John in like manner would have us survey the measure of God's love. He would have us bow in reverence or stand in worship and proclaim to mankind, "Behold, what manner of love the Father hath bestowed upon us."

In a third sense this exclamation suggests that we not only look at the fact of God's love, but that we gaze at it for a long time. It invites us to contemplate this great truth reverently and thoughtfully like we might gaze upon a masterpiece of art that charmed us and held us until its tone and its message and its meaning overwhelmed us with a new significance. We are bidden here not simply to think about it and rush out to let mundane affairs press in and monopolize us, but instead to kneel in reverence, bow down in worship, stand humbly and gaze at the fact of God's measureless passion until it melts our hearts into penitence and brings us in reverence before him.

Sometime in my hours of devotion I like to think about God and give rein to my imagination. I think of God scooping out rivers and piling up mountains and flinging continents and planets into their place and holding the destiny of nations in the palm of his hand. I think of God as the Creator and myself as the creature. Sometimes I think of God as the King of the universe and all the nations of the earth as parts of the one kingdom with one King ruling over all and myself as the subject. John, however, was not bidding us here to think about God as the Creator and ourselves as the creatures or about God as the King and ourselves as the subjects. He would have us behold a loving Father—loving to the extent that through the gift of his Son he brings us back into his favor and makes us to be his children.

Let us never forget that all effective reasoning concerning human redemption must begin with the fact of God's love. We simply cannot begin to think logically about man and his salvation until we reverently believe that God loves us—not that he will love us, but that he does love us. It is not that he will love us if and when we become good, but that he loves us now even while we are disobedient children. All effective reasoning concerning human salvation, I repeat, begins with the fact of God's love. Our prayers, our good works, our sacrifice, our faithfulness are all important, but they are secondary. There is no hope in time or eternity unless it is found in the fact that God loves us.

Over in Revelation, we find in the King James Version of the Bible this passage translated in the past tense, "Unto him that loved us." All of the revised versions use the present tense, "To him who loves us." Love is a bigger word than loved. It is a word that transcends all the rules of grammar. We cannot say God did love, he

61

does love, he will love. When we think about the love of God, all we can do is bow our heads and surrender our wills and remember that God's love forever is. We cannot think of a time when he did not love us nor conceive of a time when he will not go on loving us. John was writing here, not about a single act, but about the abiding state of the heart of God. He loves us even now, while we are indifferent and uncontrolled sinners.

A farmer once had on top of his barn a big weather vane and on top of the weather vane a sign saying, "God is love." A skeptical neighbor commented, "Bill, you mean God is love if the wind blows right."

"No, he replied, "I mean God is love whichever way the wind blows." And that is right. Recently a father whose worthless son was giving him trouble was talking with a neighbor who had no children.

"If that were my boy," said the neighbor, "I would kick him out of the house."

"If he were your boy," the father replied, "I would kick him out, too, but he happens to be my boy."

All the effective reasoning concerning human redemption begins with the fact of God's love. He loves us, and there is not a sinner anywhere, the vilest man or the most indifferent woman, who could not say as John was saying, "He loves me. He gave himself for me." Once that is established, once you can stand on that, the indifference and opposition and rejection will shrivel up. We cannot go on rebelling against the God who loves us like that.

God's love is not a general philosophic attitude. It is a personal affection. Someone said of Henry Ward Beecher, a great preacher of another generation, that he loved everybody so much he loved nobody very much. Some people think about God like that. It is not true of God that he loves everybody in such a general way that he does not love you and me in a personal way. He knows your name. He knows the street upon which you live. He knows the problems that beset you. He knows the sins that you have turned to when the strength of life is gone. His love bespeaks a personal relationship.

> I know not what the future hath
> Of marvel or surprise,
> Assured alone that life and death
> God's mercy underlies.
>
> .   .   .   .
>
> I know not where His islands lift
> Their fronded palms in air;
> I only know I cannot drift
> Beyond His love and care
> —JOHN G. WHITTIER

Four little lines by Joyce Kilmer are favorites of mine:

> Because the road was steep and long
> And through a dark and lonely land,
> God set upon my lips a song
> And put a lantern in my hand.[1]

God's love is everlasting. It does not wear out. It does not lose patience. It does not wash its hands of us. It clings to us regardless of our unworthiness.

In the twenty-seventh psalm David wrote, "When my father and my mother forsake me, then the Lord will take me up." (K.J.V.) When I read that passage as a little boy, I did not like it. I would say to myself in little boy fashion, "That's a strange God. 'When my father and my mother forsake me, then the Lord will take me

---

[1] "Love's Lantern" from *Poems, Essays and Letters* by Joyce Kilmer. Copyright 1914 by George H. Doran Company. Reprinted by permission of Doubleday & Company, Inc.

up.' He'll never get a chance to take me up because my mother and father will never forsake me."

One day at Emory College in Oxford, Georgia, the great Hebrew Christian teacher, Julius McGath, came to that passage and said, "That is not a very good translation in the King James Version. It ought to read like this, 'Should my father and my mother forsake me, then will the Lord increase his hold upon me.'"

God loves you when everybody else loves you. He will love you in fair weather or in prosperous times, but if life turns and deals you such severe blows that even your parents wash their hands of you, God comes a little closer. In the hour of life's greatest trials, he increases his hold on you. That hold is bigger than all my comparisons. No combination of words will ever adequately tell the story of his everlasting, immeasurable love for his children.

The second word I would emphasize is "us." "See what love the Father has given us." "Us" means you and me, does it not? Unworthy, unrighteous, unrepentant, unlovely—yet he loves us. I wonder if you ever tried loving somebody who did not return your affection. Those who have had the experience know that it is hard to love someone and get no response at all. As a rule you and I bestow our affection upon people who have something in them or about them that draws us to them and merits our affection. Did you ever send a gift at Christmastime to someone you knew did not like you and would not appreciate it? No, I am sure you did not. We love lovely people and bestow our affection on people of merit; we send our gifts to those who will appreciate them.

But wait. With all earnestness I remind you that God is loving us when we are not lovely. He is loving us when we are not lovable, except in the divine heart of God. He is bestowing his affection upon us when we have nothing in us to merit that affection. He sent the gift, even Christ, to a people who did not appreciate it and as extraordinary, as unlikely as it would seem, he nevertheless loves us. Let us cease our wandering, let go of our worries, turn loose our merry-go-round of trivialities, forget the pressing demands of business, and stop to "see what love the Father has given us, that we should be called children of God."

The first appointment I ever had was a circuit with seven churches on it. I lived in a little village and four miles up the railroad track was another little village. Midway between the two Mr. Bennett, a railroad section foreman, lived. His house sat on the bank of the track, and the great trains whizzed by on their way to Florida through what should have been the playground of his children. One night a man brought word that Mr. Bennett wanted me to come quickly. I hurried up the railroad tracks with the man and reached the Bennett house to discover tragedy. That afternoon, as Mrs. Bennett was in the house sweeping the floor, she heard the roar of an approaching train and looked out to see her baby sitting in the middle of the track. The mother flung the broom aside, ran out of the house, caught the baby, and gave him a tremendous push to safety, but too late to save her own life. I tried to comfort the broken-hearted husband and to say something to the children who were too young to realize the tragedy that had overtaken them. It was nearly midnight before the neighbors gathered in and I could be to myself. As I walked out into the night and looked up at the stars I said, "Lord Jesus, this is actually what you did for us."

There was an hour in your life and the life of all of us when we sat on the track of disobedience and the trains of blighted hope and withered ambitions and impending death came rushing upon us, but out of eternity came the strong hand of God pushing us back into his family. Christ gave his own life in the doing of it. Does not love so great give you pause? If we would but kneel reverently in the presence of God's love, it would work a transformation in the lives of all of us and send us singing on our way. Upon us—undone, unrighteous, unrepentant, unworthy—he has poured out his measureless love "that we should be called children of God; and so we are."

I never go to London without remembering one of the great preachers of another generation who marvelously influenced my life, G. Campbell Morgan. When Dr. Morgan would come to America, I would almost sell the coat off my back to go and hear him. I have a notebook now full of sayings I took from his lips. The church where he spent a lifetime is near Buckingham Palace, the home of Queen Elizabeth. Describing the scene in front of the palace when the grandfather of the present queen lived there, he pictured guards pacing up and down as they do now and personages of rank and authority coming to see the king. At the gate they would present their credentials, would be identified and examined, and sometimes would be denied admittance. On some mornings a little pony pulling a wicker rig bearing three happy-faced children would fly through the big gate of the palace grounds unchallenged, and the children would tumble out and rush up the stairs and down the hall into the king's private parlor. I do not need to finish the story. Formalities—pomp, ceremony, protocol, security measures—all were cast aside. These were his children. Their sonship, their daughter-hood gave them the right to the king's presence and the king's interest and the king's love. "See what love the Father has given us, that we should be called children of God";—not subjects, not slaves, but children—"and so we are." If then we are his children and he is our Father, we can never slip beyond his love and care.

Then there is another word. "Beloved, we are God's children now." Christians do not put as much radiance under that word "now" as they should. Beloved, now. Jesus said, "For this is the will of my Father, that every one sees the Son and believes in him should have eternal life." We think of everlasting life as a gift of God when we pass the judgment beyond the resurrection. Not at all. That gift is ours now; it never leaves us. We do not have to reach heaven or the judgment day to enjoy the privileges of sonship and daughterhood. Now, even now are we the sons of God.

Too many people carry their religion and it gets heavier and heavier. It ought to be carrying them. It ought not to be something to endure; it ought to be something to enjoy—now, right now. Some professing Chirstians remind me of a man with a headache. They would give anything to be rid of the ache, but they cannot spare the head. They have to have religion of some kind but have only enough to make them miserable. They are afraid to live or afraid to die without it, but the victorious, triumphant experience of being a child of the King has not yet possessed them.

Suppose I were in a strange city without a friend and without a place to stay and without a bite to eat. Unknown to me, I have in my inside pocket a ten dollar bill. Homeless and hungry and lonely though I am, this bill could never help me and never minister unto me until I discovered it. If you have religion and never know it, then you could lose it and never miss it. There is something better than a faltering hope, and Christians ought to be singing it and living it. The spirit itself beareth witness with our spirit that we are now—now—the children of God, not because we deserve to be, not because we have earned the right, but because God for Christ's sake adopted us into the family.

After John impressed upon us that we are God's children now, he began to tell us about heaven. "Beloved, we are God's children now; it does not yet appear what we shall be, but we know that when he appears we shall be like him, for we shall see him as he is." Out of an old-fashioned songbook called *Sacred Harp,* my father and mother used to sing about heaven. My father had an old-fashioned treble and my mother a beautiful alto. They drilled into my growing mind that if I got to heaven, I would find the streets all gold, the gates all pearl, and the buildings exceedingly fair. Golden streets and pearly gates would no doubt impress many a believer, but we make a mistake when we fasten our attention on our interpretation of the physical attributes of heaven. It does not matter where it is. If Jesus were to take his redeemed people into a desert, it would blossom like a rose, as would a wilderness turn into a garden, or hell into heaven. In the end the confirmation of his redeeming love is that it lasts; it brings us into his presence.

In the final verse of our text John tells us, "And every one who thus hopes in him purifies himself as he is pure." What does he hope? He cherishes the hope of being with him yonder and being like him; every man who has this hope purifies himself. He gives himself to a personal, passionate pursuit after Christ's likeness. The credential is not your church membership, but that you are trying to be more and more like him and ready for that day when we shall see him face to face. We cannot have Jesus as the type and pattern of our heavenly life unless we take him as the type and pattern of our earthly life. We cannot be willing to be like him there unless we are trying to live for him here.

One of my dear friends of another generation used to tell in his own fashion a story I have repeated many times. A scientist in Scotland armed with a powerful magnifying glass wandered alone into the highlands of Scotland. In a recess of one of the lovely Scottish hills he at length came upon the object of his search—a delicate little flower which the Scots call the heather bell, delicate and fragile and beautiful. He studied it intently under his magnifying glass so that he could see it growing in all of its glory.

Presently a shadow came over the glass, and he looked up to find standing over him a shepherd who was tending his sheep on the hillside. When the shepherd saw the flower under the glass, he exclaimed: "I'm sorry you ever showed it to me. Just think that these rude feet of mine have trod so much of it in the ground!"

If only we will look at the heart of God through the telescope of Calvary, our hearts will melt into tenderness, and we will surrender at his feet.

Hindrances to Victorious Living

"Therefore let us . . . go on to maturity."

—*Heb. 6:1*

For though by this time you ought to be teachers, you need some one to teach you again the first principles of God's word. You need milk, not solid food; for every one who lives on milk is unskillful in the word of righteousness, for he is a child. But solid food is for the mature, for those who have their faculties trained by practice to distinguish good from evil.

Therefore let us leave the elementary doctrines of Christ and go on to maturity.

—Heb. 5:12–6:1

The scriptural authority for this message is found in the initial statement in this passage. Another translation has the author of this letter telling those to whom he wrote that it is difficult to explain his message to them "because you have shown yourselves so slow to learn. For whereas, considering the time that has elapsed, you ought to be teaching others, you still need some one to teach you the very alphabet of the Divine Revelation." [1]

Nowhere in the New Testament have I found a more rewarding single book than this Letter to the Hebrews. We are not sure who

[1] *The Twentieth Century New Testament* (New York: Fleming H. Revell Co., 1909).

wrote it, but I think Paul did. We do know that it was written to a group of Hebrew people who some thirty years prior to the date of the letter had accepted Christianity. Do you realize what that step involved in the life of a Hebrew? It meant he had renounced Judaism, the religion of his fathers, had turned away from the dull, dead ritualistic round of that faith and had come to enlightenment and conviction and conversion; he had come to the point where he accepted Christ as the Messiah and as his personal Savior and Lord.

Now thirty years had gone by and these Hebrew Christians were not completely satisfied in their Christian faith. They were seriously contemplating turning away from Christianity and returning to Judaism. This letter was written for many purposes, but chiefly to save them from that step backward. It begins with the subject of revelation. "In many and various ways God spoke of old to our fathers by the prophets; but in these last days he has spoken to us by a Son, whom he appointed the heir of all things, through whom also he created the world." It takes us back across the aeons and pictures Christ as the preexistent Christ; that is, before he was born in Bethlehem's manger, he lived in heaven as the only begotten Son of the Father. Then it unfolds the old story of God's revelation of himself. Now God had spoken to them through his Son, and so the theme becomes the preeminence of Christ, the superiority of Christ over prophets and angels. It tells them that Christ is God's ultimate revelation of himself, that there is nothing beyond Christ. Its message to these Hebrew Christians is that if they were to go away from Christ back to the prophets, it would be like going away from the glaring light of the noonday sun to the flickering light of a candle.

If there is a key word in this epistle to the Hebrews, it is the little word *better*. It runs like a scarlet thread through the whole book, telling of a better revelation, of a better country, of a better faith,

71

of a better resurrection. This letter presents a series of contrasts between Judaism and Christianity. The author made no war on Judaism; he agreed that it had had its day and served its purpose and brought its revelation of God. It is well to remember that loyalty to truth as we see it does not put us under the necessity of flailing others over the head who do not see it exactly as we see it. His message was simply that Christianity is better than Judaism. So I say the book of Hebrews offers a series of contrasts between the good things of Judaism and the better things of Christianity. These Hebrew Christians were intimating that Christianity had failed them and they were about to revert to their former beliefs. As a master spiritual physician, the writer began to diagnose their trouble. He knew exactly what it was.

He was not like the doctor who was consulted by a woman whose strange disease eluded him. "Did you ever have this before?" he inquired.

"Once before," she admitted.

"Well, you've got it again," he informed her.

This diagnostician writing to the Hebrews recognized the signs and symptoms and told them that their spiritual helplessness did not grow out of the fact that Christ was not full of power but out of their failure to appropriate Christ. He reminded them that they were about to do spiritually what their forefathers had done physically. After the children of Israel had come out of Egypt, had experienced that marvelous deliverance at the Red Sea, and had been rescued from their wanderings in the wilderness, they came one day to a place called Kadeshbarnea where they were to pass over into the land of promise. As they stood on the threshold of their inheritance, fear took hold of them. Instead of marching ahead they turned back and went into the wilderness where they wrote rather a shameful chapter.

The Letter to the Hebrews pointed out that they were doing spiritually what their forefathers had done physically. They had come out of the old life. They had left Egypt, figuratively speaking. They had experienced conversion, but as Christ had tried to lead them on and upward into deeper revelation of himself, they had been too easily satisfied. The lure of the Temple and the pressure of old friends and the appeal of the old ritual had been holding them back from appropriating Christ.

They were like the little boy who rolled out of bed and hit his head on the floor in the middle of the night. His mother gathered him in her arms and said, "How in the world did you happen to fall out of the bed?"

Still sobbing, he replied, "I was sleeping too close to the getting-in place."

That is exactly what these people had been doing. They had not appropriated Christ, and if I wanted to be a critic of the church, I think I would start right there. One of the weaknesses of the church is that we are too easily satisfied in our spiritual life. We think of conversion as maturity when it is only infancy. We are converted and baptized and there we stop. The years come and go and we become critical of the church and critical of one another. The whole problem grows out of the fact that we do not walk in the light, that we do not have new understandings of his will, that we do not have new insights into his purpose, that we do not make new appropriations of his grace; we are too easily satisfied. So with these Hebrews of old. Their trouble was not that Christ had failed them, but that they had not apppropriated Christ. By this time they ought to be teachers, but instead they still needed to be taught. They ought to be leaders, but still needed to be led; they ought to be in the University of Christian Truth, but they continued to repeat their ABC's. They ought to be grown up, but they remained babies—

retarded, dwarfed, anemic, lopsided—and now wavering in their faith.

This picture is too much like too many of us to leave us comfortable. Most of us do not want a picture that looks too much like us. My disappointment must have been apparent when I looked at the proofs of my most recent pictures for the young lady who brought them out quickly said, "Bishop, we haven't touched them up yet."

I hastily replied, "Would you mind touching them up?"

After she had touched out one of the two chins and a goodly number of wrinkles, I vowed never to have my picture made again unless the photographer had a good touching-up department. Not many of us want a picture that looks exactly like us. We are not as honest as Cromwell, who had a large wart on his chin. When he sat for a portrait, he said to the artist, "Paint me just as I am, wart and all."

Unfortunately this dwarfed, anemic, self-centered group of Christians looks too much like us. They had not grown. They had stayed too close to the getting-in place. They were keeping one foot in the old camp as they feebly tried to appropriate Christ. They were babies when they ought to be grown up. Now I really know something about babies. My wife would laugh at that claim because she has reared our children while I have been out to the ends of the earth. Nevertheless I do know a little about babies and I know a great deal about church babies. Once I was the pastor of a church with 5,100 members—too many, if you ask me privately, for a single church. When some 5,000 members are banded together in one church supposedly as brothers, they may prove to be not even a company of cousins. You would be surprised to know how many babies there were among the 5,100 members of my church.

The hard fact that makes a preacher grow old ahead of his time is that the church is nearly always a field in which he must work rather than a force with which to work. We simply do not grow in grace. We do not come to have commanding stature. We are babies. Three characteristics of babies are outstanding among church babies.

First of all, babies are always jealous. What you do for one baby, you must do for the other. During World War I, when our boys were young, I thought I would buy them a soldier suit in New York. I went to Macy's and found exactly what I wanted.

"I'll take this one," I said, "and another one two sizes smaller."

The saleslady looked around and then said, "I'm sorry, sir. This is the only one I have."

"That breaks up the trade," I replied.

"Isn't this what you're looking for?" she asked.

"Yes, exactly, but I have two boys and if I brought one a soldier suit and not the other, I would have a war in my house as bad as the one in Europe. You know that I can't do that."

Babies are hardly out of the cradle before they look around to see if they are getting what is coming to them. They are always measuring themselves by other people. That is a very pronounced characteristic of spiritual babies. Mrs. A announces, "I've been in this church for twenty-five years and that woman just moved here last fall. Now they've made her president. If they can get along without me, I can get along without them," and away she goes.

Brother B gets out of humor because he was not nominated for the official board. Whenever you see a person more interested in place than service demanding his spot in the sun, I would not go so far as to say he is not Christian, but certainly you are dealing with a spiritual baby. Babies are always jealous.

Secondly, babies demand plenty of entertainment. If I had all the drums and dolls and Indian suits I have carried across these years to our children as they have grown, I could retire again from the ministry and open up a ten cent store. We are always giving babies something to entertain them. We used to have a song about spurs that jingle-jangle. What baby is not always wanting spurs that jingle-jangle? As spiritual life goes down in a congregation, the trappings of religion are apt to multiply. I have no quarrel whatever with form and order and beauty in our worship, but I happen to know that the deadest churches in this world are the most formal churches. When we get where we cannot enjoy the Word of God, where we do not eat the Word, where we are not interested in the things of the spirit, then we bring in something to dazzle us, to jingle-jangle. As spiritual life goes down, ecclesiastical machinery as a rule increases because babies demand something to entertain them.

Third, babies cannot stand much exposure. We can go to a football game in the rain or in the snow, but on prayer-meeting nights, it takes only one bucket of water to run us all in the house. We just cannot venture out in the rain or the snow.

Here is the picture, beloved. By this time we ought to be leaders, but somebody has to lead us. We ought to be teachers, but we go on reciting our ABC's. We are afraid we will get too far away from the old crowd and the old habits.

Billy Sunday once said, "If the church were as afraid of worldliness as of holiness, we would take the world for Christ in this generation." There is much truth in that statement. If you and I were to become as afraid of falling below the standard of Christ and disappointing him as we are of shocking a rather flippant, superficial age and crowd, we could have a genuine revival.

Certain trends and tendencies come into our lives like a fog. They work on us when we least suspect that we are in danger. We have made life to be easy going. We have cultivated our soft sayings about life. We are not as realistic about life as our fathers. They used to ask questions and then answer them themselves.

Bishop Kennedy once said a certain preacher was "divinely dull." When asked how he could be divinely dull, the bishop replied that no preacher could be that dull without supernatural assistance. An old English preacher in the divinely dull category was droning away when he interrupted himself to say, "And now I shall ask myself a question."

"If you do," remarked a weary brother in the congregation, "you will get a foolish answer."

Our fathers and mothers in their self-examination used to ask themselves questions which were far from dull. "Am I a soldier of the Cross?" "Can I be carried on flowery beds of ease?" They were quick to reply in terms far from foolish. "No, I must fight if I would reign." It behooves us to be realistic about trends and tendencies manifest and active in our modern life that reduce many of us to poor, pale, anemic Christians when we ought to be red-blooded and vigorous and triumphant and full of witness and power. Let me mention three of them.

First, *I think our generation is suffering from the same troubles these Hebrews experienced of old.* They had no thought of giving up religion. They were, in fact, exceedingly religious, but they had said to themselves that it would be easier to be religious after the pattern of Judaism than after the pattern of Christianity. There was a great difference. In Judaism all they had to do was get in the procession, bring a sacrifice, perform a ceremony, and go through a ritual, whereas to be a Christian they had to crucify self, they had to think, they had to stretch their minds, they had to humble themselves in the service of Christ. There is all the difference in the world in those two expressions of religion. I am afraid our generation is accenting the activities at the expense of the spring from which the expression must come.

Religion is both experience and expression. Those are the two wings of the same bird. If the bird does not have both wings he cannot fly. Some people talk about experience all the time and never mention expression; soon they lose the experience. Many people talk about expression but neglect the experience. If we try to carry on the expression of religion without the experience, the form without the substance, we grow weary after a while, throw up our hands, and cease to carry out the activities. I say they are the two wings of the same bird. It is the tendency of our time to be fussy, to be busy, to hear the roar of ecclesiastical machinery, but to neglect our private devotions. Solitude is the nursery of a full-grown soul. I have no difficulty maintaining an orthodox head if you let me be the judge of my own orthodoxy—and most of us are. The trouble is not in keeping my creed correct. Where I do have trouble is going with our Lord early in the morning, just the two of us, for a season of prayer. The expression of religion is not nearly as difficult as is the experience of putting my life and will under the mastery of his will. My one religious difficulty is the difficulty of being religious. It is so easy to put religious experience outside our activities. As with the Hebrew Christians, we find it so much easier to attend a ceremony, perform a rite, get back in the crowd, and carry out the ritual than to read the Bible or to study to show ourselves approved unto God, workmen who need not be ashamed.

This great conflict goes on all around the world today. I am not the advocate of one big church in the world. Why not? Certainly I am for Christian unity and comradeship, but if ever we have just one big church, it will tend to be so highly ritualistic that substance will be sacrificed to form and experience will wither away. We have a variety of tastes. Let us keep in mind that to be a Christian, fully oriented and victorious, is to do the works, of course, but they must be the fruits of religion and not the roots of religion —the expression of but not the substitute for spiritual experience.

My dear friend, Merton S. Rice, one of America's greatest preachers, used to say that when the first-century Christians got together, they were always talking about power. They marveled at the power that was available to them as the people of God. Now when twentieth-century Christians come together, they are always talking about problems. I would not have us say less about problems, but the two must go together. Many times during my ministry I have wished I could get the busy people to be good and the good people to be busy. I found that goal hard to attain. A host of people just bustling with activity know little about love for and loyalty to Christ. Many others seek to grasp great spiritual truths in their own inner life, but they never express these concepts in the great redemptive purposes of Christ. It is one of the tendencies of our times to be forever on the move, going here and there, but neglecting the cultivation of our spiritual life.

Second, *I think the mighty swirl of life that has come down upon us,* call it what you will, *is taking its toll of spiritual vitality.* I hardly know how to describe it. After a week or two at college, a girl wrote her mother three lines and signed the letter, "Yours in mad haste." I should have a stamp like that. I thought I would cease receiving mail upon retirement, but I am getting more than I can answer. Life is like that. Yours in mad haste.

Someone said the other day, "One has to run like 'the mischief' to stay where he is." More thoughtfully someone has commented that the race moves at such a pace that if one stops to tie his shoelaces, he will be crushed beneath the feet of the oncoming multitude. That is the kind of world in which we must live. When I talk about solitude, when I talk about contemplation, when I talk about the holy habits, when I talk about seasons of prayer, you wonder how I can be so demanding. We are in the swirl of life that has descended upon us unawares. We are caught up in a maelstrom of activity that leads to little time for all the intangibles that cultivate our minds and deepen our experiences.

One of the tragic losses of our times is what I call *the sacramental value of the family gathering.* I am not referring to prayers, but I include prayer. I mean something much bigger. The sacramental value of the family gathering rests in talking with each other, reading to each other, living with each other, growing in each other's love. Lack of appreciation of this value is in large measure responsible for nearly one out of every three marriages in America ending in divorce. We do not take time to let our marriage take root; we do not live together long enough. The first storm that hits, over goes the tree. Unquestionably the loss of the sacramental value of the family gathering is impoverishing our homelife. If I wanted to destroy America, I would attack three institutions—first of all the Christian home, then the Christian school, and then the Christian church. If we want to know what kind of a world we will have fifty years from now, we have only to see what kind of homes we have, what kind of schools we have, and what kind of churches we have. The world of tomorrow is being fashioned now. If we allow these three fundamental institutions to suffer, then we imperil all that is basic in our national life.

Something is happening to the Christian home. Wherever I go the average home is not a home; it is a lodging house. The average dining room is not a dining room; it is a lunch counter. We do go home occasionally; the car has to be parked somewhere. Home used to be a place to which we were eager to go, but now it is too often a place from which to go. This change is taking its toll. It is taking its toll in our reading. Not many of us have time to tackle a good sizable book; we read the digest, and now I see there is a digest of the digest. We hardly have time for this digest and by next spring there will be a digest of the digest of the digest. We are so everlastingly on the go that we do not take time to nourish the intellect, let alone the spirit.

We do not take time to dig out information, to think through the great issues, and our minds become cluttered with nonsense. If we read of church matters at all, we are inclined to read articles critical of the church instead of those that uphold the church. In the headlong rush of today's world, intellectual apathy stalks our path, and we are impoverished mentally and spiritually. Again I repeat, solitude is the nursery of a full-grown soul, and unless we take time for the sanctities of our faith, the holy habits, we cannot grow in grace and in the knowledge of the Lord Jesus Christ.

This fearful rush is taking its toll of preaching. Never have I given a preacher the slightest encouragement to be lazy, but when will our laymen discover that preacher cannot be out on the streets six days a week and then come into his pulpit on Sunday morning with the dew of heaven on his brow and the voice of the prophet of God on his lips? A man has to study if he is to preach. Yet we increase our demands on his time and keep him forever going somewhere. Then we are critical of the Word as he presents it and turn to popular themes. That is the world in which we live. Life swirls all about us. It is high time that we make time for the holy habits of religion, for reading the church press, for the things that contribute mental vigor and an understanding of what our church is about. Unless we make time, these other forces will overwhelm us.

Third, *our generation has an exaggerated emphasis upon pleasure.* There is a place in a Christian's life for that which cheers and entertains and amuses and re-creates. That is the word—re-creation.

We Americans have quit saying re-creation; we say recreation, and most of the activities we call recreation just wreck. Pleasure is supposed to be a re-creating process that brings us back to the routine tasks stronger in every way. The daily duties are the main consideration; the pleasure is only temporary diversion to help us keep fit for the regular occupation. It is always secondary. Too often we reverse the process; we play and then we work if there is any time left. Let me repeat, there is a place in a Christian's life for that which cheers and entertains. I do not have a long-faced, unhappy philosophy of Christian life. For fifty-two years now I have been preaching and I have never had a dull day at it. It has been a romantic and heavenly experience, and I am the last one to spread gloom. There is a place in your life and mine for pleasure, for wholesome entertainment, for cheer.

After giving her heart to Christ, a little girl went home skipping and singing. Her grandfather told her if she was going to be a Christian, she would have to give up all the skipping and singing. She retreated to the yard where an old retired mule stood with his head over the fence. Reaching up, she stroked its face and said, "You must be a Christian mule. You look just like my grandfather."

Where did this gloomy concept of Christian behavior originate? Somebody evidently told us a long time ago that it was pious to be long-faced and devilish to be happy. We believed it. We have never quite dispelled this false impression. As a matter of fact, it is pious to be happy, to have a cheerful outlook, to believe in God, and it is devilish to go around peddling our woes all the time.

A boyhood schoolmate of mine always had a sore finger, and his mother could get more rag around that one finger than you would ever believe. I would meet him coming down the road and say, "Lloyd, how's your finger?" and he would start unwrapping the bandage. He would no more than get it back on again, though not as good as his mother had it, before someone else would ask about the finger and off would come the rag once more. He stayed in the fifth grade three years. How can a fellow show off his sore finger all the time and get ahead with his study books? Many people are like that. They are always saying how bad things are. They never tell how good they might be if Christ had his way. In curbing an exaggerated emphasis on pleasure, we need not go to the other extreme.

This matter of appropriate diversion and wholesome activities is not to be settled by laws. A law is man made. It can be repealed. What might be a fair law in one place could be an unfair law in another place. Laws are not the answer. Some early churchmen made a list once, years ago, and said everything on this side you can do and everything on that side you cannot do. Then new things kept coming up that were not on the bad list and so they said they are not prohibited and we will do them. A principle is involved here. You can take a thing within itself perfectly harmless and let it grow and grow and grow in your life until it crowds out more important things. When that happens, it is not innocent anymore; it is harmful. As a boy I used to borrow a knife and play mumblety-peg. Most folks now are not old enough to know what mumblety-peg is, but you throw an open jackknife in the sand and the score is reckoned by the way the blade lands. That used to be a thrilling boy's game. It is perfectly innocent. You would not object if I took some preachers around on the sunny side of my house and had a game of mumblety-peg, would you? A harmless pastime. If, however, mumblety-peg became so interesting, so fascinating that we allowed it to crowd out our study, our routine duties, and our daily tasks, then it would no longer be harmless. We make such a tragic mistake when we label this good, that bad, arbitrarily. We can let a good thing grow and grow and grow until it crowds out better things, and then our lives are out of balance.

I do not object to a man being a member of a lodge. When the lodge horn is blowing and the prayer-meeting bell is ringing—except that we do not have these any more—and he hears the lodge horn but cannot hear the prayer-meeting bell, then something is wrong. The lodge might not be bad, but his life is out of balance. I do not object to a woman belonging to a club, but if the club gets all of her time and all of her enthusiasm and all of her strength and the church society has to drag her in, then her life is out of balance. If we are not on guard, we can let that which within itself is harmless grow, grow, grow until it crowds out essentials, ceases to be harmless and becomes downright harmful. God and church and home and duty must always take precedence; the time for play comes after we have put first things first.

The tendency of our generation to substitute the activities of religion for the experience of religion, the mighty swirl of life to let down upon us until we are always on the go, the necessity to quest for pleasure—these all reflect the times in which we live and affect us all. I know good people, nice people, who cannot spend an evening at home by themselves. They do not know how to read; they do not know how to carry on a good conversation. They just bore themselves or seek escape in television programs. The tendency to substitute the performance of religion for the experience of religion, the mighty swirl of life that leaves us but little time or place for the cultivation of our spiritual interests, the exaggerated emphasis on pleasure that lets secondary things supersede primary things—are these not three danger signals along the way that warn us to hurry on to maturity? Whenever you see the word "therefore" in the Bible, always stand at attention. "Therefore," wrote the author of the Letter to the Hebrews, if the kind of an approach you have made has brought you to this impotent, unhappy state of spiritual life, if failure to grow in grace has reduced you to babyhood, therefore, leave the beginnings. Give up your ABC's. Give up milk for solid food, which "is for the mature, for those who have their faculties trained by practice to distinguish good from evil. Therefore let us leave the elementary doctrines of Christ and go on to maturity."

Henry Drummond said a long time ago that what the church needs is not more of us but a better brand of us. While I would like to see millions of new people come into the church, first of all I would like to see you and me come to a new allegiance, to a new appreciation, to a new love, to a new reverence for Christ, to a new passion for his will. If we could have a revival of genuine spirituality in our hearts, then the outside world would come to see what had happened to us. Therefore, leaving the elementary principles, the beginnings, let us go on unto perfection. Let us press forward to maturity.

God's Willingness to Forgive and Forget Our Sins

> *"I, I am He,*
> *who blots out your transgressions . . . ,*
> *and I will not remember your sins."*
>
> —Isa. 43:25

If you were to go into a store tomorrow with some thought of purchasing a diamond, the chances are that before the jeweler brought out the stones for your inspection, he would spread a black cloth on the counter or the table before you and then place the diamonds upon it. I have not had much experience with diamonds, but I presume that the black background brings out the beauty and the brilliance and the strength of the stone to a better advantage. I do know that the promise which is my text as found in Isa. 43:25 is a diamond all the more glorious and all the more extraordinary when you look at it resting as it does against a very, very dark background.

God spoke directly here to the children of Israel and, of course, through them to us. Let me remind you that they were God's chosen people, not chosen in the sense that they were to go to heaven no matter how they lived, not chosen for salvation, but chosen for service. They were chosen in that God had designated them to become a righteous, ministering nation, a people to whom he could speak and through whom he could speak to other nations. Nevertheless Israel went to pieces on the rock of spiritual selfishness, and God's plan for his people and God's purpose for the world through them came to miserable failure because of their disobedience.

In the verses immediately preceding this glorious text (Isa. 43:22-24), God brought against this people several specific indictments before he made the diamond promise in which are revealed his amazing grace and his measureless mercy. You will never see the beauty of the text, you will never understand its redeeming love unless you are willing to take a little time to look at its dark background; unless you spread out this black cloth, the promise will never break upon your souls. Let us look hurriedly but carefully at these indictments.

The first one is in the twenty-second verse, "Yet you did not call upon me." This approach always intrigues me. When God set out to enumerate the sins of this people, the first sin he put down was that they had not prayed. Do not let me leave with you the impression that they had utterly forsworn all their religious interests. They had not cast off religion altogether; they had not forgotten that Jehovah reigned in the heavens and that they must give an account to him. Despite this formal acknowledgment, in a period of prosperity and expansion and security and health they had lost their sense of dependence upon God and they had turned their confidence upon themselves. The years had come and gone, and they had not prayed. In the imagination of their wicked minds, in the deceitfulness of their rebellious hearts, they had forgotten that God was the source and the sustainer of life. They had forgotten that in God we live and move and have our being and without God we cannot live and we cannot move and we cannot have our being. They had grown independent. They had accepted a secular interpretation of life and imagined that they could manage life without the mercy and without the grace and without the help of God.

They were too much like too many of us to leave us comfortable. In fact every one of these indictments spread on this black cloth applies to us with devastating aptness.

I dare say that you may have arisen this morning unmindful of God's watchful care over you through the unconsciousness of last night's sleep. You awoke to this beautiful day with its fragrance and sunshine and to a life far better than almost any other people in the world ever enjoyed. Yet not once this day have you been on your knees in grateful recognition of God as the source and the sustainer of life. I would not indict you. I simply say that you are in health and you have a degree of prosperity, and life has dealt kindly with you; but an overwhelming sense of your utter dependence upon him gets lost. You go day in and day out without the humble heart, without the bended knee, without the trusting soul, and God speaks to you now as he spoke to Israel of old, saying, "Yet you did not call upon me." Your neglect breaks the heart of God. Suppose a baby came to your house, and when at last the child reached the stage that he should recognize you and love you, all you got was a blank stare. That would be tragedy, unspeakable tragedy, and it would break the heart of loving parents. Likewise it breaks the heart of God that you take all of his rich gifts and never look back in grateful recognition or bend the knee or humble the heart to say thank you.

I heard the other day of two Irishmen out in a boat. A storm swept down upon them, the waves were running high, and it looked like they might be lost. Pat said, "Mike, I'll pray while you row." Mike rowed with all his might while Pat began to tell God what he could expect from the two of them. Presently, Mike shouted, "Pat, don't promise too much. I believe I see land." God gives us a little help and a little prosperity, and we think we see land; the days and the years come and go, and we do not call upon him. In the deceitfulness of our wicked hearts we imagine that we can live and move and prosper without his blessing.

When I ask people, as I most certainly do at the end of the service, to seek the forgiveness of God, I am talking not simply to those who have made a shipwreck of life, not alone to someone who has horrified his neighbor, but also to those who have merely allowed a purely secular interpretation of life to dominate them until their sense of dependence upon God has somehow been lost. That is the first sin.

Second, in the twenty-third verse God said, "You have not . . . honored me with your sacrifice." Watch the inevitable sequence unfold. The religious life of Israel was expressed by bringing to the temple a sacrifice and offering it up to God. That is what you and I would call the performance of the religious duty of God's chosen people. That was the holy habit of their faith, to bring a sacrifice. They recognized God; they worshiped God by the offering of a sacrifice. As soon as they quit praying, they broke down in the performance of their duty; the holy habits of their faith were neglected. "You have not . . . honored me with your sacrifices." Of course they were not loyal and faithful to a God to whom they never prayed and whose mercy they did not recognize and upon whose grace they did not depend. They had utterly broken down in the performance of their religious duties, and again they were like too many of us. How often have we neglected these holy habits of our faith? How often has our pew in the church been empty when the preacher and God desperately needed us? How often have we lacked in the support of the great redemptive enterprises? How true is this statement, "You have not . . . honored me"? What sacrifices have we made? We have broken down, I repeat, as did the ancient Israelites; too many of us are too much like them to allow us to be comfortable and complacent.

The third indictment God brought was the loss of spirit; the tone and temper and manner of their lives had now become not one whit different from the tone and spirit and temper of the people of other nations round about them who made no profession of faith in Jehovah. Their behavior had changed to conform to life around them; instead of being kind and patient and forgiving, they were unkind, impatient, and unforgiving. They had lapsed until there was no difference between them as the people of God and the other people who made no profession. Again one could say a great deal here about how conformity and convention have invaded the life of the best of us. All too often we lack courage to speak up, to take his side, to share his ideals, and to follow him in his redemptive way.

The fourth indictment is in the twenty-fourth verse:

> But you have burdened me with your sins,
>   you have wearied me with your iniquities.

If my dear mother, who is in heaven, were here to translate that passage in her own way, she would say, "You have made me to put up with your sins." God's people had not sinned once and ceased, but over and over and over again until God said, "You have made me to put up with your sins." Furthermore, "You have wearied me with your iniquities." If my mother were to translate that, she would say, "I am threadbare." I have heard her say to me more than once, "Go away and let me rest. I'm worn out; I'm threadbare." That was what God was saying. This sinning, this deliberate, malicious, willful, conscious transgression of the law of God had occurred so often and had continued so long that God said, "You have worn me threadbare—burdened me with your sins— wearied me with your iniquities." Of the sins of omission and the sins of commission, I do not know which are the more deadly. The sins of commission stab the soul to death. The sins of omission starve the soul to death.

Beloved, reflected in that picture of ancient Israel we see ourselves. The best of us, I am afraid, have not always acknowledged God as the source and sustainer of life. The best of us have broken down in the holy habits of our faith. The best of us have not always been distinctively and intelligently committed and convinced disciples of his. Some of us, too many of us, have willfully and repeatedly transgressed his law until this picture of God's people portrayed by Isaiah is likewise your picture and my picture. One of the difficulties in the way of experimental religion is that we do not like to admit that we are sinners. We have narrowed this whole definition of sin down to some overt act that horrifies everybody. We do not think of sin except as some willful transgression that shocks the community. We think if we do not shock the community or violate some known law, we do not need God's forgiveness.

Do you not remember what Jesus said about the coming of the Holy Spirit? "And when he comes, he will convince the world of sin." What kind of sin? "Of sin, because they do not believe in me." There is no sin for which we need forgiveness more than the sin of self-confidence and independence and a secular interpretation of life that robs us of an overwhelming sense of our need of his mercy and his help. We are sinners.

Harry Denman, Secretary of the General Board of Evangelism for The Methodist Church, who was my colleague in Birmingham, has a way of going up to perfect strangers and asking them to pray for him. In a big department store in an American city he once said to a strange saleslady, "Will you pray for me?"

"Yes," she replied. "What kind of trouble are you in?" We do not think we have to pray—we do not think we need God—until life devastates us.

Before us on the black cloth are the indictments. God's chosen people had not prayed. They had broken down in the performance of their duty. They had not manifested the right spirit. They had deliberately transgressed his law. Because that picture fits me and fits you, I want to know what God does with people like that, I want to know what God says to people like that. Does he wash his hands of them? Does he drop them into oblivion? Does he shut the door of mercy? Does he tell them their chance is gone? No, a thousand times no.

In the very next verse, scintillating in all its beauty against the background of the black cloth, is the wonderful promise:

> I, I am He,
>> who blots out your transgressions for my own sake,
>> and I will not remember your sins.

God's challenge was, "Put me in remembrance." Change your ways. Cast off your indifference. Renew your vows. Resume your holy habits. Repent of your sins. Then, "I, [even] I am He" who will blot out all of this miserable record. "Thus says the Lord who made you," whose image is upon you, and whose Son was to die for you, "I will not remember your sins." That is the way God treats any man or woman who wants to be good. As long as we are proud and conceited and independent and refuse to bow our heads and acknowledge our sins, not even God can do anything for us except prolong the day of his mercy. When we quit comparing ourselves with each other, when we stand in the white light of his holiness and discover the extent of our failure to conform to his will, when we are overwhelmed with the sense of our own undoing and when we begin to confess our sins then:

> I, I am He,
> who blots out your transgressions . . .
> and I will not remember your sins.

That is the diamond upon the black cloth—the priceless gem of an everlasting promise of forgiveness.

Some illustration, some figure of speech I would hold before you that will make this entire story of God's willingness and eagerness to forgive and forget our sins come alive until it melts our hearts into penitence and brings us repentant to our knees. First of all, this is a chemical transaction. Here are your page and mine in the Book of Life, spotted and stained and unsightly, soiled with the sins of omission and the sins of commission. It is all there—the failure to pray, the failure to serve, the failure to behave as becomes the man of God. Do what we will, we cannot erase it; the record is there. When we admit that we are sinners and come acknowledging.

> Thou must save, and Thou alone:
> In my hand no price I bring;
> Simply to thy cross I cling.

Then Christ does for us that which we cannot do for ourselves. Another hymn puts it:

> Jesus paid it all,
> All to Him I owe;
> Sin has left a crimson stain,
> He wash'd it white as snow.

If we would come with a penitent heart, confessing an overwhelming sense of our need of his measureless mercy, the crimson tide of his shed blood would pass over your page and mine and carry away in its crimson flood every stain and spot.

93

The reconciliation with God is likewise a commercial transaction, imperfect as the figure of speech may be to convey a message about the love of God. On your page and mine in the Book of Life the account grows larger and larger with the passing of the days. This sin of omission, that sin of commission, failure to do this or that— they all add up. The truth is that we are all paupers; we are all bankrupt when left to ourselves. If we say we have no sin, we are deceiving ourselves. When the light of God's grace turns upon us, we discover that we are sinners and that the account against us grows larger and larger. If we had all the gold of the Rockefellers and the diamonds of every mine, if we had the gems of every sea and the cattle upon a thousand hills, if we had the wealth of every nation and could put it down as payment against the debt we owe God, we would still be paupers. We cannot pay it by ourselves. Once we cease trusting in ourselves and begin to acknowledge our need of Christ, that change of heart will be put to our credit and will balance the account. God will write your name and mine at the top of a new page, and the old account will be wiped out. That is what Paul had in mind when he said, "There is therefore now no condemnation for those who are in Christ Jesus." You cannot storm the gate of heaven and demand eternal life on the pretext of faithfulness and good works. It is in the name of Christ, with him confessing you before the Father, that the debt is paid in full and the account balanced. He will work in your life here and now the miracle of release and renewal and send you out to live a new life, with a new purpose and a new victory, in a new world. He will blot out your transgressions and not remember your sins.

Well do I remember the first morning I went to school. Tiny little boy that I was, I walked the three miles down the sandy road from home in town to the schoolhouse and back again in the afternoon. Why the trustees located the school so far from town was beyond my comprehension then and is now. It was hot September, and my mother had me bundled up as for Arctic wastes. I trudged along carrying my three-story lunch in a little tin bucket—biscuits on the bottom, bacon in the middle, and a little cup of syrup on top. If at recess you have never made a hole in a cold biscuit with your finger, filled it with syrup, and then feasted, I pity you.

The new teacher at the one-room country schoolhouse was a lovely young widow, married the year before, whose husband had lived only a few months. She was dressed in deep black, which in fact she continued to wear until she went away to heaven a few years ago. She had another name, of course, but I met her that morning as Miss Mittye and can hardly remember her surname now. She was beautiful. I fell in love with her before recess and from that moment never fell out; I loved her all her life and continue to cherish her memory. Her influence over my life was profound— simply beyond telling. I make my letters now as she taught me. What I learned in college I have forgotten, but I have not forgotten what Miss Mittye taught me. The lasting impression she made upon my childish mind and her unfailing love and devotion I can never overestimate.

All that I am or have been able to do in the world has come as the result of the love and guidance and loyalty of at least four good women. My mother was a very superior woman with an English background. She did not tell me she was English, but the traces of English ancestry were evident. She was without formal education, although liberally endowed with natural gifts and a woman of great wisdom. As I stood at her grave again the other day, my debt to her broke over me with a new realization. She was only thirty-seven when she went away to be with God, having borne five children, of whom I was the oldest. I could never overestimate the influence of my mother's faith and example.

The Council of Bishops the other day presented to Mrs. Moore and me a silver bowl on the occasion of our golden wedding anniversary—which I had forgotten. I telephoned her and said, "Mother, the bishops have given us a silver bowl."

"What for?" she inquired.

"We've been married for fifty years."

"That must have been your first wife," she responded. "I haven't been married to you *that* long."

It had indeed been fifty years since we had married very early in life for she is the only wife I have ever had. An inquisitive woman once asked me, "Bishop, have you ever regretted marrying so early in life?"

"Yes, indeed," I replied, amused to see her come to attention anticipating a choice bit of gossip. "I have regretted it a long time for I love my wife so much that I regret I wasn't born married to her. I'm just sorry I missed those first years." Whatever my role has been—as circuit rider or bishop in the church or ambassador of Methodism to the ends of earth—her love and loyalty and good sense have been more than half the battle. She led me to Christ; the winsomeness of her own life made me want to be a Christian.

Then there is a little woman living still down in South Georgia. The first charge I ever had consisted of seven country churches and there was only one family on the charge with any formal education or with any money. When conference time came, this gracious lady said, "Don't you think you ought to go to college?" I had been her preacher for twelve months; she knew I ought to go somewhere.

"What can I do about college with a wife and two babies?" I asked.

"My husband and I will send you a small gift each month if you want to go," she replied.

"We're on our way," was my joyful response.

We moved up to Oxford, Georgia, where I attended Emory College. We paid four dollars a month rent and had a few left for food and the other needs of the four of us. We had no wearing apparel to buy for friends gave us a barrel of clothing once a year. Sometimes I have driven hundreds of miles to sit at the feet of these dear friends. I can never thank them enough. Their gift of a few hundred dollars each year was the bridge of destiny over which my whole ministry moved from the obscurity of that circuit to whatever else I have been able to do in this world. It is such a shame that some people I know waste enough on one party to give some hungry-minded student a chance at an education.

My mother, my wife, my benefactors—and now back to my teacher. At school the last subject Miss Mittye assigned us in the afternoon was arithmetic. I have never been good in that particular subject. Certainly arithmetic was my Waterloo. Miss Mittye would put the examples—I think we called them sums—on the blackboard and we would copy them on our slates. When we thought we had the answers, we would walk up to her desk, put the slates down and go home. She would grade them, and we would pick them up the next morning and see the grades. I always wanted to please her. Every afternoon I would start out with great determination, mindful that correct answers and neatness both counted. On the first example I would get the lines straight and the answer right, and usually on the second one. By the time I would get to the third, I would remember I had one more biscuit left in my little bucket, and the lines would be crooked and the answer incorrect. Before I could get to the fourth one, a ball game would be in the making outside and I would miss that one. Then as I hurried to get away, my hands would perspire and I would almost rub out the ones I did have right. There may be a slight exaggeration here, but I honestly never walked up and put my slate down that I did not wish I could wipe it clean and do the sums all over again to please my beloved teacher.

Is there not an analogy here with the slate of life? Did you ever get the lines crooked? Did you ever fail to recognize God? Did you ever break down the holy habits of your faith? Did you ever manifest the wrong spirit? Did you never sin? I am appealing to people who have quit comparing themselves with each other, who stand in the light of God and who see how utterly they have failed him. How does the record stand on your slate? I rejoice to tell you that if you will come with your head bowed and your heart humble and tell him about your sins, if you will confess your sins, he is faithful and just to forgive them. He will wipe out the whole miserable business. With a clean slate you can start life all over again from this hour. You can say with Paul, "There is therefore now no condemnation." Jesus Christ will do for you and for me that which we cannot do for ourselves.

In the last line of the text is this glorious assurance, "and I will not remember your sins." When God forgives us, he not only takes the record of our sins out of his book, but also takes the remembrance of them out of his mind and out of his memory. When people grow old and begin to forget, we pity them. But remember that one of the divine attributes of God is to forget. When God forgives, he forgets. He will take the prodigal back and forget that he ever wandered. The prodigal will not forget, but God will treat him as if he had never wandered. "As far as the east is from the west," said the Psalmist, "so far does he remove our transgressions from us," and in the closing words of our text, "I will not remember your sins." What is your response to God's willingness and eagerness to forgive and forget? Sometimes I think if God were to treat me harshly, if he were to pick me up without loving me and cast me out into eternity, I could bear even eternity away from him if I could only remember that I never had a chance. There is enough of the stoic in me that I would shout back to God and say, "Unjust —unfair! But if I were ever to wake up in eternity away from God and remember that God did not send me there, if I were ever to come to the realization that I went there over love like his, I could not stand it. You do not have to debate with me as to what hell will be like. I do not know. If it is nothing more than the consciousness that I would never yield to love like this—God's infinite love that forgives and forgets—that would be hell itself.

When you go over to London, go down to St. Paul's Cathedral. There in the main sanctuary, just to the right of the high altar, is the lovely painting by Holman Hunt, "The Light of the World." He gave the first painting to Oxford University, specifying that no fee ever be charged to see it, but when he found a fee was being charged, he painted a replica of it and hung it in St. Paul's Cathedral, where it hangs today in all its beauty.

Years ago before the cinema, as the English say, had come to England, a lecturer with colored slides on religious subjects came one night to Manchester to show his pictures in a great hall crowded with miners and their families. When Hunt's famous picture of the waiting Christ knocking at the door that would not yield came upon the screen, he stood quietly and let the marvelous painting speak for itself. Presently a child's voice broke the silence.

"Daddy," she asked, "Why don't they let him in?"

"I don't know," he whispered. "You must be quiet."

She was quiet for a moment and then, overcome with anxiety, repeated, "Daddy, why don't they let him in?"

"Hush," he murmured. "I don't know." She was quiet as long as a little girl could be under such circumstances. Then she cried out so that everybody in the great hall heard her.

"Daddy, I know why they don't let him in. I know why. They

must live in the back of the house." She could not imagine people keeping such a lovely Savior waiting unless they were beyond the reach of his call.

That is the tragedy in your life and mine. We are not vicious; we are not antireligious. We do not expect to die without God, but when Christ comes knocking at the door of our heart, too many of us live in the back of the house. We simply are not at home to God. As we meditate upon God's willingness and eagerness to forgive and forget our sins, let us fling open the door and yield to his love and let him become the great lover of our soul.

The Greatest Danger in One's Life

"But supposing him to be in the company they went a day's journey."
—*Luke* 2:44

The broad foundation upon which I base this sermon is a fascinating story taken from the boyhood of Jesus (Luke 2:41-51). The curtains are pulled back, and we are permitted to look in upon the growing life of our Savior. The Gospels have much to say about the birth of Jesus, his public ministry, his atoning death, and his victorious resurrection and ascension, but they are strangely silent concerning his boyhood. Here we are permitted to glimpse what someone has called "the hidden years of Nazareth." We can be glad that too much tradition, fable, and fiction have not accumulated concerning his youth. The scene upon which we look pictures an incident of the hidden years.

I am confident that Jesus was a normal boy and also that when he grew to manhood he was strong, vigorous, and attractive. I have never believed that he was quite as gray of face and sad of countenance as the artists have painted him. His face must have mirrored his strong, dominant personality as well as his compassion for humanity. One day after Jesus had grown to manhood, he was in the midst of a great crowd. Some little children pulled away from their parents, slipped up to stand by the Savior, and then to climb upon his knee and snuggle within his arms. They felt perfectly at home in his presence. Little children do not search out the long-faced, solemn man.

Our story concerns Jesus as a twelve-year-old boy. The time had come for the annual pilgrimage from Nazareth, his home, to Jerusalem, eighty miles distant. The journey was to be made overland by a slow and difficult process, but Jesus was no doubt eager for it. I do not imagine that a single bird singing on a bough or a rabbit skipping across the road, if rabbits there were in Palestine at that time, escaped the attention of this normal, keen-minded, high-spirited boy.

On arrival in Jerusalem, Joseph, Mary, and all the elders joined in the great feast of the Passover, which lasts for several days. The feast over, the time had come to retrace their steps; they must travel the long road back to Nazareth. Eager to get home, they undoubtedly got an early start that first morning. How early we usually start off the first day of a long journey. I remember the time I took my family for a motor trip through the Northwest and the Rockies. We decided it was easier to keep the children in the car when they were impatient to be on the way and so we left at five-thirty the first day of our trip. To use a southern colloquialism, we were "journey proud," and so dawn found us on the high road. The next morning our starting time was an hour later, and each morning thereafter we got a later start.

That first morning, after their long absence, Joseph and Mary and all their friends and relatives must have left early and traveled steadily on toward Nazareth. When the day was far spent, the shadows were lengthening, and the sun was dropping behind the horizon, the party stopped. Perhaps they erected rude tents and made camp alongside the road.

Then Mary said, "Joseph, I don't remember having seen Jesus

this livelong day. I don't think he's been with us since we left Jerusalem."

"Now, Mother," answered Joseph, manlike, "don't worry about him. He's with some of the neighbors in the party, I'm sure."

But Mary, motherlike, did worry. "Well, it is night now, and his place is here in the tent with us. I want you to go find him and bring him to me."

So Joseph went looking for Jesus. I can imagine that he went to Matthew's tent, asking, "Matthew, is Jesus with you?"

"No, I haven't seen him today," Matthew replied. "Perhaps he's in John's tent."

"John, do you have Jesus with you?"

"No, Joseph, it's been two or three days since I recall having seen him. Isn't he in the tent with you and Mary?"

Joseph, concerned by now, hurried from tent to tent, earnestly seeking Jesus, only to discover that he was not in the company at all.

A great preacher of another generation, with tremendous spiritual insight, had this to say concerning our story, "What you have here is the story of the most unlikely person in all the world, losing Jesus in the most unlikely place."

The last person you would ever think of forgetting him for even a moment would be his mother, and the last place in which you can imagine other matters crowding him out of her affection and interest would be at the Temple. Nevertheless this is our story; the most unlikely person in all the world lost Jesus in the most unlikely place. We must be fair to Mary and not intimate that she gained the consent of her mind to go even one day without him. She had no thought of leaving him behind, no thought of traveling on the homeward journey without his presence. She knew she had not seen him that day; she knew she had not heard the laughter of his voice; she knew his arms had not been about her neck. There is one word in the lesson which is the key to the tragedy from which came all the bitter regret and the frantic haste to return to Jerusalem. One word—"but supposing him to be in the company they went a day's journey." So much had to be done, so many neighbors were needing assistance, and so many people seeking advice that life became full of bustling activity and Mary traveled an entire day *supposing* Jesus to be somewhere in the company. She did not choose to forget him, but all these extraneous affairs, not bad, not vicious, but necessary and legitimate matters crowded in upon her. For a day, at least, she lived under the mastery of earthly things which cluttered her life, her attention, and her heart, so that this day she left Jesus to care for himself.

Someday I shall preach a sermon on "The Tyranny of Things"— legitimate, necessary things. We Americans bristle when talked to about the "tyranny of kings" and we say we do not like kings. At least we do not like the idea of living under the rule of a king. I was in Oslo recently when the King of Norway entered a great hall and we stood to our feet. We respect kings, but are thankful our country is not a kingdom and we protest vigorously against being so ruled. Then why do we become willing slaves to the tyranny of things? Things dominate us, monopolize us, deceive our reason, drug our conscience, and carry us away, not in willful choice, but in neglect of the imperishable values of life. That is what happened to Mary. Things crept in upon her, like a thief in the night, and life became so crowded with other duties that she went a day's journey without Jesus. Now that the tent was made ready, the sun had gone down and darkness was about her, she wanted him, but he was not there. All she had concerning the presence of her dear Son, the Savior of the world, was a supposition. She supposed him to be in the company.

May I ask you with a rather insistent earnestness what life has been doing to you? No one ever lived through a more trying period of history than we of this generation. For fifty years, since the beginning of World War I, we have lived at the center of a catastrophic convulsion. Life has been hectic and crowded and full of demands comparable to those made on Joseph and Mary. Have you, too, lost him? I know you have not disowned him like Peter, nor sold him like Judas. I know you have not cast aside your Bible and turned atheist. I know you have not walked out of the church and declared your emancipation from its creeds. But have you been going, day in and day out, busy with a thousand and one things, supposing Jesus to be in the company?

Did you ever know a better day, religiously, than this one? Did you ever have more joy in the service of the church than you are having now? Has life stolen out of your religious nature something that was once very precious? Have you settled down to a sort of garrison duty while you live in the experience of another day? Have you lost him? Are you singing that hymn that William Cowper wrote many years ago:

> Where is the blessedness I knew,
> When first I saw the Lord?
> Where is the soul-refreshing view
> Of Jesus and His word?

Is nothing left but a faltering hope, a dead supposition, or do you have the living presence of our Lord in your heart?

There is a story in the fourth chapter of John's Gospel about a woman you remember well. That poor woman, with her soiled life, made some interesting observations, among them two that were very penetrating. She turned to view her past wistfully and longingly, saying, "Our fathers worshiped on this mountain." This was history; this was memory; this was the past. Then she turned, with

105

FIGHT ON! FEAR NOT!

even more wistfulness, to look toward the future and said, "I know that Messiah is coming (he who is called Christ); when he comes, he will show us all things." This was hope. Here we see the only mountain peaks in her entire makeup, a dim memory, and a distant hope. This woman, in the valley of her depravity, was talking face to face with the Son of God, but had no capacity to recognize him. Some of us are like her. There are many professing Christians who when you speak to them about religious experience, about the vitality of faith, about the love for the Savior can come no closer than the faith of our fathers.

Harry Denman came south to preach in a revival. A dear friend of mine, who is a very gracious lady, invied him to be her guest. When she showed him to his room, she remarked, "Dr. Denman, this is the room in which my grandmother prayed."

"I am not interested in where your grandmother prayed," Harry responded in his tender fashion. "Where do you pray?" I have an interest in your grandparents, but I must ask with insistence, have you lost him? What has life been doing to you?

There is another story concerning the night Jesus was being tried and the people were condemning him. The record tells us that "Peter went out on the porch." There was nothing happening on the porch, for the trial was on the inside, but Peter went out on the porch. He edged away from it all. Have you been doing as Peter did? One of the perils of our time is the sacrifice of moral ideals to popular standards and the subjection of personal conviction to current opinions. We are not in danger of atheism for atheism has gone out of style. Our danger lies in a purely secular interpretation of life that salutes religion but does not live itself out in creative fellowship and in happy reconciliation with the Savior of the world.

In the book of Revelation there is the story of an entire church to which this kind of tragedy occurred. You know the scripture, "Behold, I stand at the door and knock." These words were not spoken to a single stubborn sinner but to the members of an entire congregation. Jesus was on the outside with the door closed while they stayed on the inside. They were talking about him, preaching about him, singing about him, but they would not let him come in. They were never so proud of themselves as after they had put him out. I imagine they had a conference. Such a meeting is not documented in the Bible, but you have to read with a sanctified imagination if you truly want to see what is there. This congregation, once they had put him and his demands on the outside, no doubt had a conference and someone offered a resolution. It must have read "Whereas." I never heard of a resolution that did not begin with this word. Whereas is a word so overused that I am aggravated by it. I am sure this was a long resolution composed by a proud, self-satisfied, professing Christian. It might well have read:

WHEREAS, ours is one of the best known churches in this city; and

WHEREAS, we have a well-trained and entertaining minister; and

WHEREAS, our budget has been oversubscribed; and

WHEREAS, we are known for the best music in town, and

WHEREAS, we number in our membership many of the most influential, social, political, and business leaders of the country; therefore be it

RESOLVED, That in our opinion we are the one and only exemplary church.

This is a picture of a church having the clatter of ecclesiastical machinery, with all the terminology of religion, busily engaged in voting itself a resolution of commendation when Christ was on the outside. Its members were proud of themselves and frankly stated that they were rich and had need of nothing. Imagine a church declaring it did not need anything. Think of a church sufficient unto itself.

What did Jesus do? He pushed the door of that church open and said, "You are not rich; you are poor. You cannot see your way spiritually for you are blind. You are not clothed in fine raiment, but naked." He told this church four things its members must do before they could recover and recapture the vitality of their faith, four steps back to spiritual recovery.

First, they were to *remember*. In the last few years, I have discovered how often in the Bible God uses the memory for a spiritual purpose. Remember, remember, remember! I wish I knew more about the memory. I do know that without it life would be blank to everything except the sensation of the present moment. By the memory process we can make the past live on and can journey backward in time. We can relive life, and memory can sweeten and soften events for us.

God turns to the church, without condemnation, and says, " 'Remember then from what you have fallen.' Remember when we were together in such blessed intimacy when I was at the center and when you loved me, when you had the experience and the expression of religion. Let the memory of those better days woo you away from this bustling activity, back to love and devotion."

From the standpoint of this world's gods, I was reared in a poor home. My father was a section foreman on a railroad, and his salary was forty-five dollars a month. Five children, my mother, and father lived on this small sum. Two or three years ago the church took our simple house, repaired it, and made a memorial of it. There is nothing of which I am more proud. The house was so unadorned in my boyhood, and we had so little that it may seem surprising we were so happy. I wonder if our generation can understand happiness under those circumstances. The average American thinks that the only way to be happy is to get more goods. The way to become truly happy is to reduce your wants and get into the right relationship with God. We were materially poor, but we were happy.

I remember the day a man drove up to our house with an organ in his wagon. We purchased this instrument, and he put it in our spare room. Then he played a very appropriate tune, an old gospel hymn called "Looking This Way." We bought it for five dollars down and five dollars a month, and he was looking our way every month for his payment until I was almost grown. There seemed to be more mirror than organ, and in about six months our musical contraption developed asthma and I almost pumped my life away trying to keep enough wind in it. My sister learned to play the hymns, and we would stand grouped about the instrument and sing. I can hear my mother now:

> We are on our way to Canaans land
> We're on our way to a pilgrim band
> Divinely guided day by day;
> We're on our way,
> We're on our way.

A long time ago she found the land about which she sang. How sweet and fragrant and happy were those days. Do you have a memory like that? If you just live in a big house, look at your bankbook, and ride in a fast automobile, if you have no hearthstone for your affections and no memories to bless and reward, then you are poor indeed. What do you think about in retrospect? Do you recall a praying father, a holy mother, and the sacredness—the sacramental value—of family gatherings? A memory like that should woo you from this indifferent life you are living and bring you back to the simplicities and the sanctities of better days. Sunday was

God's day in our home, the Bible God's book, the church God's house, and the preacher God's man; and we were happy. Far too many with similar memories have been swept by the currents of life from their old moorings.

The second admonition Jesus gave to the church was to *repent*. When Joseph and Mary found Jesus, his mother said to him, "Behold, thy father and I have sought thee sorrowing"—"have been looking for you anxiously." If they had merely said, "Too bad. We've lost the boy, but we must get home," the tragedy would have been multiplied. But they turned around and sought him sorrowing. The church, mentioned in the book of Revelation, could not just open the door and say, "Come back." They had to seek him sorrowing, look for him anxiously, repent of their trust in themselves and of their multiple activities and of their rejection of the Savior of the world.

We should not say less to this present generation about faith, but we should say more about repentance. We make a great mistake when we delegate a secondary place to Jesus and put our trust in the work of our own hands. A woman laughingly said to me, "I'm not the woman I used to be." I have heard men say, "Well, I was active in the church, but I'm not anymore." It is as though they were telling this to me with no more concern than they would state they had a bad cold. That is the language of damnation. If one can laugh off his spiritual decline and laugh about the loss of his faith and the fact that he does not love God as he once did, then that is the deepening darkness of his soul gone blind, the slow, creeping paralysis of his heart and mind. Mary and Joseph found him when they sought him sorrowing, and so can we.

The third admonition was that they should *return*. Joseph and Mary found him where they had left him. Perhaps you say, when speaking about an hour when darkness creeps over the earth, "The sun has gone down." But the sun does not go down. The sun is still shining, but now that we have turned away from it, darkness is over the earth. Tomorrow morning, when the earth turns back, the sun will still be shining and will fill the world full of light and beauty again. We should avoid conformity. One of the perils of our time, I would emphasize again, is the sacrifice of moral ideals to popular standards and the subjection of Christian convictions to current opinions. We must reject such practices and return to him. Joseph and Mary could have conformed to the itinerary of the party, but every hour would have separated them farther from Christ. They found him when they retraced their steps and they found him exactly where they had left him.

If I have intimated that Christ leaves us, I would dispel that idea. He does not leave us. We leave him, and this question of spiritual renewal is not bringing God down, but bringing ourselves up. It is not saying long prayers until God restores his people; it is putting ourselves in harmony with his will. It is not new vows we need; it is the revitalization of those we took a long time ago.

The last admonition was to *repeat*. I may have spoken sarcastically about the work of the self-satisfied church members after they had put Christ out. Perhaps I should have said simply that they were busy. When Christ is put back at the center, he does not say quit working; he does not say give up the time-consuming activities. His command is to "do the works you did at first." He tells them to let their works, their service be the fruits of religion rather than the roots of religion, an expression of love for Christ rather than a substitute for devotion.

There are but four steps: Remember! Repent! Return! Repeat! So the story ends by telling us that Joseph and Mary found him where they had left him.

A beautiful daughter came to live in our home until diphtheria took her away one Easter season and left a wound in our hearts through which some of our blood has been pouring ever since. We lived in Texas at that time and every morning, earlier than her father wished to awaken, little Dorothy would come to pull the covers back and with her infectious laughter say, "Get up, Daddy, it's morning." This is one of my fine memories, hearing my baby say, "It's morning." Let us go back to our old vows; let us cease speculating and begin to give the world the spectacle of a devout spirit and obedient will. Then it will be morning in our souls. God has not left us; we have left him and we can find him again when we seek him in penitence.

In another generation when couples married, it used to be fashionable for them to go to Niagara Falls on their honeymoon. You who have been there will recall the cataracts back on the lake which, ultimately, become the falls. If you go back far enough from the falls, you can go boating in comparative safety. There is always the slow imperceptible movement of the water, but far enough back you can breast the currents and row your boat. If, however you stop rowing and allow your boat to drift with that slow steady movement of the waters, danger threatens. If you ever allow your boat to drift beyond a certain little island, it is said that no human strength can save you and you must go plunging over the falls to death. On one side, safety, on the other, destruction. Someone has named the little island "Redemption Point." Once beyond, there is no redemption.

To follow Jesus Christ afar off, without deliberate purpose, to be caught in the swirl of life and follow him at a great distance is a tragedy, but to become conscious of our loss and fail to seek his presence is more than earthly tragedy. It is the deepening darkness of one gone blind, the slow paralysis of heart and mind.

The Tragedy of Stopping Short

"He went away."

—*Matt. 19:22*

We read in Matt. 19:16-22 one of the most instructive and rewarding stories to come out of the earthly ministry of our Savior. Jesus
was preaching—perhaps at some crossroads—talking to the people
about God and life and redemption and duty and immortality.
When the young man who, but for Jesus, is the chief character in
this story came that way with his entourage, I am sure he stopped
at first out of idle curiosity to see what this itinerant religious
teacher was saying to the people.

Notice who he was. He was the rich young ruler. He had all that
you and I strive for and that we think accompanies greatness and
success in this earthly life. He had political power; he had commercial prestige; he had social standing; he had charming personality; he had moral uprightness. He had nearly everything we
ordinarily associate with success, and he stopped, I think, out of idle
curiosity to hear the teachings of this man.

As he stood there listening to Jesus, he found his mind and his
soul going out, not only in interest, but in response to what Jesus
was saying. After he stood at a distance for awhile, he gathered his
royal robes about him and came running to prostrate himself at the

113

feet of Jesus. Matthew did not say he came running, but Mark, in recounting the same incident, said he came running and knelt before him.

Do you not rather like the way he went about it? I am not saying you must do it that way, but I like his earnestness. I like his urgency. I like his enthusiasm. I grow weary of those persons who have so much energy and so much enthusiasm and so much drive for everything else in the world that they seem to have little or none left for the church. We are overworking our emotions in America today in every realm of life except in the realm of religion. "Oh," you say, "Bishop, we don't want to be fanatics." Neither do I want you to be, but a person does not become a fanatic because he has too much religion. He is a fanatic because he does not channel his un-reasoning zeal properly. It will not hurt you to have a little more religion. I like the way that young man came seeking—his intensity, his earnestness. He came running!

As a young preacher I was even more intense than I am now. A woman in a Southern city who heard me several times said, "Will you read a book if I send it around to your hotel?" "Yes," I said, "I will." Her chauffeur brought it to me. He had on a uniform that looked like some South American general, and the book was tied up in tissue paper and baby-blue ribbon. Wondering what this woman wanted me to read, I finally got down to the book. Its title was *Calm Thyself*. That I did not do then and that I shall not do now. I do not want to be as calm as some Methodists I know until I am dead.

The young man came running and prostrated himself at the feet of Jesus. Then by the very first question he asked, he proved that he did not know how to enter the Christian life. It is remarkable how much ignorance we can display sometimes when we try to talk about something we do not understand. That first question proved unmistakably that he had not learned how to begin the Christian life. Did you notice what he said? "Teacher, what good deed must I do, to have eternal life?" In other words, "What charity shall I support? What good works shall I perform? What shall I pile up as a sort of merit until, as a reward for what I have done, I may pound on the gate of heaven and demand to be admitted because I have been morally upright and have been busy?" That was his mistake, you see. "What good deed must I do?"

You will forget much that I say, but remember this, *you do not become a Christian by doing so much good work and being so faithful that heaven and eternal life come as a reward.* That is not the way the experience comes. You become a Christian when you say quietly and openly, "In my hand no price I bring," because if your hands are full of moral uprightness and full of pride and full of good works, then you have no empty hand with which to cling to the cross. You say, "In my hand no price I bring. I have nothing to offer. Simply to thy cross I cling." The way to become a Christian is to admit that you need God's love and Christ's power, and then let Christ do for you that which you cannot do for yourself. This was the young ruler's mistake. "What good deed must I do?"

Jesus—always a wise and understanding teacher—named six of the Ten Commandments, and the young man said, "All these I have observed; what do I still lack?" Many of us think that we shall come to heaven as a reward for simple moral uprightness and keeping commandments. If a man could "do" his way into the kingdom of God, this man would have been in. Jesus was leading him along, letting him discover that he was on the wrong track, that he was trying to attain eternal life as a reward for his own performance or his own behavior.

Then Jesus turned to the main issue and said, "Sell what you possess and give to the poor, and you will have treasure in heaven;

and come, follow me." Let me come into your life. When I come in, I bring life, for "I am the way, and the truth, and the life; no one comes to the Father, but by me." There the road forked for this young man. There life became dramatic for him. Several times in this series of sermons I have remarked that life flows along for us as peacefully as a river for ten, twenty, thirty years; then suddenly it becomes dramatic. It is full of fury and foam, and we are called upon to make great choices, to swear allegiances, and to take our side. That is what happened to this man. When Jesus said, "Sell what you possess . . . ; and come, follow me," life became dramatic, and this young man looked at his possessions and then looked at Jesus. He thought about his own hungry heart and looked again. Then he put his foot down—watch it—and made as tragic a decision as you can find anywhere in this Bible. He said in effect, "I thought I wanted eternal life, I thought I wanted to be a Christian, I thought I wanted to enroll as one of your disciples; but if that's the price, if I must pay that much for it, I'm not interested." He arose from his knees and "went away sorrowful; for he had great possessions."

The old-time preachers had an illustration about a little boy who came to his father one day with his hand caught in a jar, his fist tightly clenched. After repeated futile attempts to get the hand out of the jar, the father said, "If your hand went in, it's bound to come out. Put your hands just like mine; straighten your fingers." "If I do that," the boy quickly replied, "I'll drop my nickel."

Many people talk about their intellectual difficulty. The real difficulty is not in the intellect. It is in the surrendered will. It is willingness to confess him. It is willingness to enlist in his service, to do what he wants. Jesus said, "Sell what you possess . . . ; and come, follow me." The rich young ruler looked at his possessions and looked at Jesus; then "he went away sorrowful."

Think of all this young man has to answer for when he comes

at last to the judgment of God, as we all will and must; I hope you will never forget that. If you will remember three great truths, you can never be totally irreligious: First, you came out of the creative hand of God. Second, you live under and are subject to the law of God. Third, you go back to God for examination and judgment. We all will.

Picture this young man as he comes to the end of his earthly pilgrimage and stands in the white light of God's presence for judgment. Not only must he give an account to God for the sins of commission, for the acts of wrongdoing, but he must also give an account for all he might have done if he had said yes instead of no that day. He might have written a Gospel like Matthew or Mark or Luke or John. He might have gone back to his closest friends and turned all of them to Christ. He might have wielded an influence all over that country which would have set the kingdom of God on its way; but all that he might have done came to naught when he decided, "The price of my own surrender is too much. I won't pay it."

Tenderly I would remind you that an accounting will likewise be required of you and me. Let us remember the stewardship of influence, of example. I am not given to wild assertions, but I dare say that if every man who reads these words would make a complete and irrevocable dedication of himself to Christ, he would find that before the end of this year three or four or half-a-dozen other men would follow him into the church. Now suppose he does not. Suppose he stays away. Suppose he refuses to make the decision. At the end of the way when the books are opened, it will not be some sin that horrified everybody for which he must answer; it will be simply the wasting of his influence, the failure on his part to use his influence over those men for Christ. The same is true for each woman—lovely, charming, and winsome—who, if she would but come to Christ and give all of her beauty and winsomeness to him, could bring all her friends into the Christian life. Do not be unmindful of the stewardship of example.

This rich young ruler went away. I never read that passage without wanting to ask openly, "Where did he go?" He went away. Where? Where does anybody go when he walks out on God? What kind of home will a man have for his soul if he will not live in the house of God? "Oh," you say, "Bishop, you've already told us. He had houses and friends and success. He had everything that one needs to be happy." Wait a minute. He had them all, but his approach to the Master indicated clearly that he was not really happy even before he came to Christ. If he could not be satisfied before the command of Christ had broken over his mind and over his heart, he certainly could not be satisfied thereafter.

As a growing little boy, I used to beg my mother for the old broom—not that I intended to sweep anything, but it had such a nice long handle. I would cut the broom straws away, cut a notch in the top end of the handle, get a red string out of the bureau drawer, tie it in that notch and then admire my creation. It was no longer a broomstick. It was a fine Kentucky thoroughbred. I wish you could have seen that horse—distended nostrils, flowing mane, magnificent stance. He would have won the Derby any year had he been entered. I nearly rode myself to death down the sandy road atop that Kentucky thoroughbred. All this out of a broomstick. Then I took a cornstalk, shaped it up a bit, and it became a sword in my hand. The troop trains were coming by, and a soldier stuck his head out of the window to wave to my sister. His hat fell off into the ditch. I got it, fastened the leather strap under my chin, and looked in the mirror. A little Georgia crackerboy no more, I was now a general in the American Army. Do not laugh at me—I was a real general. I got on my horse and rode up and down with my sword in my hand.

One morning I looked down the road from our house and discovered that the Spanish army had moved up overnight and had camped almost in our yard. The pine forest that had always been there was gone, and Spanish troops were there instead. It dawned on me that the destiny of this nation depended on that battle, and the battle depended on my leadership. I called my soldiers to attention and as I rode up and down on my fine horse, I told them how critical the situation was and asked them what I could expect of them. They saluted and assured me, "You can count on the last one of us dying in his place or winning this battle." Brandishing my cornstalk sword, I led them right into the battle. I cut off the heads of Spaniards, stabbed them, mowed them down, and won the war. I ought to be getting a hero's reward instead of being a Methodist preacher.

What am I trying to illustrate? There was an hour in my life when I was abundantly satisfied. I was perfectly content to ride a broomstick, but not anymore. I got into an automobile one day and rode off. I boarded a jet plane in Tokyo and flew the Pacific in fourteen hours from Yokohama to Los Angeles at between six and seven hundred miles an hour. Imagine me getting off a jet plane, mounting a broomstick, and galloping up the road. I am not too proud to undertake such an adventure—although my figure does not suit it very well—but it will not work now. There is good psychology here, and there is religion here, too, good religion.

There doubtless was an hour in the life of the rich young ruler when he had a form of satisfaction from material possessions and friends and gaiety and success. At least he had something he thought was satisfaction; but now that his soul was aroused, now that his mind was concerned, now that the call of God was upon him, and

119

now that Christ was speaking to him, he could never again have anything like true satisfaction. You see he had tasted the better thing, and when you have tasted the better thing you can never be satisfied with the lesser thing. So he went away to disappointment, to choked ideals, to thwarted plans, to unuttered longings, to unrealized ideals, to unfilled ambitions, to an unhappy existence. He went to all of that because in the one hour of his soul's history when he was face to face with the call of God and the command of Christ, there was something he loved more than he loved Christ. That is the tragedy of stopping short. He was interested, he was seeking, he was earnest, but when that something was revealed and he learned what had to go before Christ could come, he decided, "I love that more than I love Christ."

Somewhere years ago, I saw a picture portraying a paved highway stretching back into the distance as far as the eye could see. On that highway, a mass of men and women, young and old, kings and beggars, pressed forward. In the mad scramble, the strong were climbing over the weak, children were being crushed to death, and that surging multitude, climbing, pushing and pulling, came on. The road made a sudden turn and then continued until it disappeared in a huge yawning chasm. Where the road turned, there stood a rough, crude wooden cross on which was hanging the Son of God. His hands were outstretched to embrace this crowd; but they refused his salvation, and in their madness, in their folly, the people hastened along down the road, swung around the bend, and still running and pulling and climbing, rushed on until they dropped over the precipice into the abyss. The Cross they passed by, unheeding. Underneath that picture was a haunting word that I shall never forget, "Tragedy, tragedy of it all, there is nothing yonder." The masses were hungry, they were seeking for something, but they ran by the source of satisfaction and the Savior of the world.

When they reached the end of the road of their own choosing, what they thought would be heaven became hell; what they thought would be a mountain became an awful precipice; what they thought would be a crown upon their head became a halter around their neck. "Tragedy of it all, there was nothing yonder," nothing yonder.

We preachers think of it as a tragedy for one to come under the influence of a religious meeting and have his emotions stirred, his desires quickened, and his interest in divine truths stimulated, only to go out of the house of God after the service and let this tide of the Spirit pass as the sweet music dies out upon his ears and this appeal of an earnest preacher no longer challenge him—to do nothing. That is the tragedy—the tragedy of it all. There is no other name for it.

Even so, the supreme tragedy in your life will come when you reach the end of the road of your own choosing, the road that you elected to follow rather than to walk with Christ and discover there is nothing there. There is no sanity, there is no security, there is no satisfaction, there is no salvation. "Tragedy of it all, there is nothing yonder."

Take a good look now at this young man about whom we have studied. He was a charming fellow. He had much in him that Jesus admired, and Jesus wanted him very much for his kingdom. Picture him as he got to his feet and walked away. When he walked out of the presence of Christ that morning, he walked into oblivion. We never hear of him again. He appears not another time in the pages of the Holy Book. "He went away"—to blighted hope, to withered ambition, to choked ideals, to unuttered longings, to unrealized capacities, because in the hour of decision there was something he loved more than the command of Christ.

The life he lived was not life at all, and the life you will live if you have rejected Christ will not be life, but thin and pale and meager existence, maybe coarse and vulgar, but it will not be life. It will be the deepening darkness of a soul gone blind. It will be a slow, creeping, fatal paralysis of your heart and of your mind.

"And he went away."

The Ministry of Memory

> *"And you shall remember all the way which the Lord your God has led you."*
>
> —*Deut. 8:2*

Traveling across my state a short while ago, weary and eager for sleep, I stopped toward the end of a strenuous day at a hotel in a small town. As the night wore on, I heard the town clock in the courthouse across the street strike ten and eleven and twelve and then one. When it was about to strike two, my patience was gone and my religion in grave danger. I decided to get up and read the Bible. There I found for the first time the text which serves as the scriptural authority for this message, "And you shall remember all the way which the Lord your God has led you." Of course I had read it before, but without full appreciation of its significance. As I contemplated these words, I discovered afresh that memory is a gift of God and that it has been given to us for a spiritual purpose. Over and over and over again as we read the Word of God, we discover how often God uses the memory to call the people back to himself.

The whole book of Deuteronomy falls into that plan. It was written, of course, long after the occurrence of the events which are recorded in it. Its purpose was to show the Israelites how good life had been, how full, when they had walked before God in obedience, and how tragically poor and miserable it had become when they turned away from the service of God. The writer was trying to call them back to their faithfulness, to their devotion, by reminding them of God's goodness in the past. By that memory he was seeking to bring them back to nobler living and higher service. This is but one illustration of God's use of the memory.

In a preceding chapter I mentioned a church whose members had wandered away from Christ, an excellent example of backsliding. When God began to deal with that church, the first step he proposed was to remember—"Remember then from what you have fallen." His plea was that they let the memory of those better days call them back to his service and to his side. Again when the rich man lifted up his eyes in torment and asked for help, the one word God was saying to him was, "Remember." God is constantly calling his people to remembrance and, by stirring our memory, bringing us back to his side and preparing us for greater issues and for nobler living.

As I approached the hour of my official retirement, I wrote down what I wanted to say to my conferences and to my brethren when I stood at the end of my active ministry. A book in my library by a distinguished English statesman, entitled *Old Men Forget,* caught my eye and I read it. It was interesting, but I said to myself, "Old men—but this one. I remember." So I wrote my valedictory address under the title "I Remember." Memory is God's gift to us and is to be used for a spiritual purpose.

If we did not have this faculty we call memory, everything that has gone before or that might come after the present moment would be a blank to us. By the use of the memory, the past can be made to live on, but how ghastly life becomes when the mind is filled with bad memories. What could be more tragic than to wander so far away from God that we have only a misspent life to review?

What could be richer and more satisfying than to reflect on God's mercies, to remember how he has led us all the way?

Tell me what you remember most easily and I will tell you what kind of person you are. Tell me what you keep stored up in your memory and I will know fairly well whether you are coarse or cultured, whether you are scholarly or vulgar. What you treasure and keep as the permanent possession of memory is a good indication of what kind of person you are.

In the passage of scripture before us, the eighth chapter of Deuteronomy, God would focus the memory of his people on his mercy. He would remind them to dwell upon four experiences in their national life that should call them away from their wanderings and bring them back to his service.

The first one is specified in the fourteenth verse of this chapter from which the text is taken. They were to remember "the Lord your God, who brought you out of the land of Egypt, out of the house of bondage." Later they were admonished to observe the Passover"—that all the days of your life you may remember the day when you came out of the land of Egypt" (Deut. 16:3). Now what day was that? That was their birthday as a nation. In retrospect they were to dwell upon their origin and ever be mindful of the miraculous deliverance as they came out of Egyptian bondage at the Red Sea when God brought them through and made out of them a great nation. If they would but fasten their attention upon that day, inevitably they would be filled with the sense of their original and inexpressible debt to God. Their deliverance was not by their own strength but by God's guidance. It was God's miracle that brought them out of bondage, and if they would only fasten their attention on that episode in their national life, they could not escape a sense of their original and inexpressible debt to God. It would rob them of their own self-sufficiency and of any idea that they had created themselves or made out of themselves a great nation.

Green, the English historian, wrote at the time of the great Protestant revival that the English people "had become the people of one book and that book was the Bible." As I pointed out in an earlier chapter, a revival had opened the Bible to plain people for the first time, and as they read it, they discovered their God-given rights. The virus of freedom got into their blood, and they began to talk about freedom of mind and freedom of conscience and freedom of press and freedom of work. We Americans accept these freedoms as our due and do not always remember how we came to be inoculated with the freedom virus. Our precious heritage came out of the revival of evangelical religion that had opened this Bible in which men discovered, almost for the first time, that they were created by God, that they lived under his law, that there was such a thing as sacredness of personality, and that they were the children of destiny. This virus of freedom from state and freedom from councils and freedom from an oppressive church got into their blood, and America was born. It would be good for America in this day of her boasted strength, of her national superiority, of her proud possessions if we who claim her for our own would drop to our knees and remember that it was not our cleverness nor our strength, but it was the hand of God that brought us up out of Egypt.

The second reminder is in the text. "And you shall remember all the way"—all the way—"which the Lord your God has led you." After the Israelites had safely crossed the Red Sea, if they had been disposed to march straight ahead, they doubtless could have reached the promised land in forty days, but it took them forty years. Those may have seemed wasted years, but now the prophet of God told them, "And you shall remember all the way which the Lord your

God has led you." Even during the long years of wandering in the wilderness, God was using their seeming adversity for his purpose. He was building bone and blood and muscle and purpose into their life so that forever they could be a righteous ministering nation. The wilderness had a lesson—to develop a people for all subsequent history.

"All the way" means that we must recognize God's leadership, we must recognize God's love and guidance at the place where it is hardest to recognize it, or we will not recognize it at any place. If we do not associate God with the valley, we certainly will not associate him with the mountaintop. If we do not let him be our God in the hour of adversity, we will not recognize him as our God in prosperity. He must be the God of the valley as well as the God of the mountaintop. At this point many of us break down. We associate God with deliverance, with prosperity, with joy. We do not always remember that he is still leading when we walk through the valley of the shadow of death—that he is the God of all the way.

When I was a student at the old Emory College at Oxford, one of my professors was Dr. Edgar Johnson. No man ever stretched my little mind more than this humble but brilliant man, and I took every course he offered. I even attended his Sunday-school class. If he had offered cooking, I would have taken that because everything he said I wanted to hear. He was a wise and godly man. One day death came to his home. His little eight-year-old daughter slipped from this world and was put away in God's acre.

The following Sunday morning, Dr. Johnson came to teach his Sunday-school class over in the college church. The subject of the lesson—or the golden text as we used to say—was, "And we know that all things work together for good to them that love God." I wondered what this honest man, this spiritual man would do with that kind of text when he had just buried his little girl, but he made no reference whatever to his sorrow.

Picking up the lesson sheet, he said: " 'And we know that all things work together for good to them that love God.' Young gentlemen, you must read this carefully. One of the important words here is the word 'All.' 'All things work.' I do not believe that you could take each and every single incident in your life and separate it from the rest of your life and say that it by itself was for the glory of God or for your good. There are some experiences that hardly fall in that category, but God's overarching purpose is about us and over us, and when all of life has been lived and God finally puts together the end result, it will be to his glory and our good." All things—not just simply one sorrow, but God's continuing purpose, the ultimate result—all things are to glorify him and work out to our good.

Recently I crossed the Atlantic once again on the Queen Mary, a proud and majestic vessel. It is an enormous ship, but if you were to break it up and throw it, bit by bit, into the Atlantic Ocean, every particle would go to the bottom. Put it together in a symmetrical whole and it becomes a proud, majestic vessel; it floats, and it goes on its way through wind and weather. There is a lesson for us here.

We must associate God not simply with the mountaintop, but with the valley, not simply with our successes, but with our sorrows. Nothing reveals the depth, the quality of our faith so much as how we react to adversity or sorrow. As a pastor, I have seen one woman bury her baby and become embittered and cynical and stay away from church and throw away her faith. I have seen another woman bury her baby and, after a period of mourning, come back with a radiance we had not seen in her face before and with a triumph in her spirit that only those who believe profoundly in God could ever have. It is all the way; it is not simply when we go into the promised land. God associates himself also with the wilderness wanderings, the hour of adversity, the experience we cannot understand; and what seems to be a devastating reverse is made to redound to his glory and our good.

When I was a very young preacher, I was privileged to hear Colonel Bringle speak. In his youth he had gone out of Harvard with honors, not to a post in official Washington as is the vogue today, but to join the Salvation Army. He was standing on a street corner in Brooklyn soon afterward when a drunken loafer picked up a brick and hit him in the head. The young Harvard man suffered a concussion and was hospitalized for months. During his convalescence he wrote a little book about the size of the New Testament entitled *Helps to Holiness*. Later he added four volumes, and these devotional books, translated into several languages, sold in great numbers around the world.

I heard the Colonel when he was very old relate this brick-throwing incident. Then he said something I shall never forget, "My young brethren, if there had never been a brick, there never would have been a book."

Remember—remember all the way. Even such an experience as Colonel Bringle related was turned to his good, to the inspiration of millions, and to the glory of God. That is the lesson—all the way, not simply in joy but in sorrow, not simply in success but in adversity. Even in the darkest experiences of life, let memory hold sway.

The third reminder is in verse eighteen. "You shall remember the Lord your God, for it is he who gives you power to get wealth." God wanted to make great a people. He wanted them to attain stature that would forever stamp them as a righteous, ministering nation. They were to remember in prosperous times that it was God who gave them power to get wealth. Strangely enough the tendency of success is to cause us to forget God. You would think that if we

129

were half conscious, we would recognize that God has been good to us and we would worship the Giver, but success tends to cause us to forget God. That is the tendency of our age. The great evil of our time is this secularism, this independence, this idea that we can manage life, this notion conceived in the deceitfulness and the wickedness of our own hearts that we are the source and sustainer of life.

Wherever I go, I am asked to meet this or that distinguished citizen who is usually described as "an independent man." I acknowledge the introduction, but I do not believe a word about this independence. There are no independent men, and this spirit of independence that we have allowed to develop here in America is the last station this side of atheism. When we think that we can manage life, when we simply worship God one hour in the week but do not hold him in awe as the source and sustainer of life, then we can easily, if our prosperity continues, slip from that state into atheism. Independence, I say, is the last station this side of atheism.

We are not independent of the forces of nature. Ask the people who were in the wake of recent storms. How helpless we are when nature goes on a rampage. I came out of New York some years ago on the Queen Elizabeth looking toward a speedy but restful voyage across the Atlantic. Right down at the mouth of the harbor, a patch of fog held us prisoner for eleven hours. All of man's glory and vaunted power shrivel in the face of nature. We are not independent of nature.

We are not independent of our neighbors. If you think you are, then let illness, a long illness, come and they do not come about you. Oh, how you need their sympathy and understanding.

No, we are not independent. This business of independence is a myth, a fallacy. It is foolishness, and certainly we are not independent of God. Even the house in which we live, the automobile we drive, and the money we have in the bank, we owe to God for it was he who gave us strength to acquire them all. We are only his stewards. "You shall remember the Lord your God, for it is he who gives you power to get wealth." Nevertheless, too many of us, now that we think we understand ourselves, do not care to remember God's will for us. This atheistic attitude has become atmospheric in our day—we prefer to think that in our own strength we have accomplished and acquired all.

A rich man was very sick when two of his friends met. One of them said, "Bill's pretty sick."

"Yes, he's a very rich man, isn't he?" replied the other.

"Yes, he is."

"Well, if he dies, he can't take it with him."

"Then he won't go," quickly responded the one who knew him very well.

But he did go, and the shroud in which they put this rich man to rest did not have a single pocket. How enamored we become of this world's goods, of the passing show; how much affection and pride of possession we lavish on the temporal.

The only real values in your life and mine are inward values. Anything that is external is not ours. We may claim it. We may enjoy it for a time, but anything that is not inside us is not a real possession. Take education. Train the mind of a child in school, instruct him in truth and uprightness at home, and that schooling becomes a part of the warp and woof of his whole life. Nobody can take it from him. Take religion, which has to do with character. No one can rob him of his early religious training; he must relinquish it. When we emerge into maturity and become blinded by earthly success and bewitched by a little position, when we forget that it was God who gave us the strength and the opportunity and

131

that we are only stewards, we all too often do relinquish it and find ourselves adrift religiously.

When a rich man dies, the frequent query is, "How much did he leave?" The only reply is that he left it all. And so do we. When a rich man took his life here in America a few years ago, many wondered why, but an earnest Christian friend said it was because he had no "invisible resources." We get so enamored of the visible resources that we can tabulate and put in the bank and pile in a house that we are prone to lose ourselves in pride of attainment and take all the credit. When we do, we are adrift religiously. "You shall remember the Lord your God, for it is he who gives you power to get wealth."

The fourth reminder is over in the seventh verse of the ninth chapter. "Remember and do not forget how you provoked the Lord your God to wrath in the wilderness." In the history of God's chosen people there had been days filled with evil. The forty monotonous years in the wilderness were monumental in wickedness. There had been anger in their heart. There had been rebellion in their spirit, and there had been disgust all about them. Now when God would redeem them through memory, his plea was, "Remember and do not forget." Not that he would have them brood over the past, not that he would wear them down with the memory of their sins; but they were to remember their sins and remember the days of their rebellion and anger as reminders of God's mercy, of how he had forgiven them and blessed them and strengthened them. To think of their sins was to remember God's mercy; to think of their anger was to remember God's pain. So with us. That is a part of our redemption, not a morbid looking back, not a brooding that keeps us always looking down, but an assurance that we were once sinners and now are saved by grace. Memory can overwhelm us with the realization of God's mercy.

By recalling these four great experiences in their national history, God's people were to keep ever fresh in their memory God's mercy. Likewise we are to remember the day when we came out of the land of Egypt, the day when we crossed the Red Sea, the day when God gave us this nation, the day of our personal conversion. Let us remember all the way his unceasing mercy, his watch care, his guidance in all the experiences of life. Let us never forget that it was the Lord our God who gave us the power to get wealth. Let us remember how he deals with us in the hour of our sin.

When in London, I never fail to visit Wesley's Chapel. There Methodism's founder lived and labored and died. It is said that when John Wesley died, he left four things: a silver spoon, a worn-out clergyman's coat, a badly abused reputation, and The Methodist Church. Nevertheless down in Westminster Abbey a tablet to him has a place of honor, and the man who could not preach except on his father's tombstone is now revered. John Wesley takes his place with Paul and Augustine and Luther in the great procession. I always go to his Chapel and wander around, as I did again recently.

Then, if I am by myself, I wander across the street over into the cemetery, Bunn Hill Field, which has been there since the sixteenth century. Thousands of people have been buried there, and I like to wander alone among the tombstones. I do not want to stay, but I like to go. I would rather read the epitaphs than some of the books that cost me much money. I usually tip the caretaker so that he will not follow me. The other day I once more had my own little pilgrimage and stood again at the grave of Susanna Wesley—mother of Methodism. Then I wandered over to the grave of John Bunyan, whose *Pilgrim's Progress,* next to the Bible, has been read by more people than any book in all history. From there I went over to the grave of Defoe, the author of *Robinson Crusoe,* a favorite of favorites

133

in my boyhood. As usual, I ended my pilgrimage at the grave of Isaac Watts who wrote:

> When I survey the wondrous cross
>> On which the Prince of Glory died,
> My richest gain I count but loss,
>> And pour contempt on all my pride.

When he surveyed, when he remembered, when he contemplated the cross on which the Prince of Glory died, when he saw what he was and what he did, Watts poured contempt on all his pride; all his independence and self-sufficiency shriveled. In this immortal hymn, he expressed how memory mirrored for him the message of the cross and the thought of God's mercy until at last:

> Were the whole realm of nature mine,
>> That were an offering far too small;
> Love so amazing, so divine,
>> Demands my soul, my life, my all.

Even in our kind of world, could we not find five minutes this day and every day—just five minutes—in which to contemplate reverently God's mercy in our individual lives? It seems very little to ask for the reward it would yield. If we would remember—remember all the way—the tenderness, the patience, the goodness of God and would count our blessings, our hearts would melt into penitence and gratitude, and we would find his service not a drudgery but a dear delight.

Finally, Brethren*

"Finally, brethren, farewell. Be perfect, be of good comfort, be of one mind, live in peace; and the God of love and peace shall be with you."
—II Cor. 13:11 K.J.V.

When one comes to the hour of retirement and undertakes to express his gratitude for the gracious words and generous help of colleagues and friends, he speaks under severe limitations. There is always the temptation to become historical and recite some of the stirring events with which one has been associated or to linger lovingly upon the names of dear companions of the way. To do either would require time which is not available. I have therefore chosen to put my valedictory in this written form. It is gratefully dedicated to my comrades of the ministry—the busy and loyal laymen, the consecrated women, and our dedicated youth. The strength of our Methodism is found in the hearts of those who bow at our altars, love our doctrines, and delight in the service of our Savior.

Memory is the gift of God and should be used for a spiritual purpose. By its use we are able to recall what the Lord has done for us, and are thereby conscripted to nobler living and higher service. As

* This address was delivered to the Southeastern Jurisdictional Conference of The Methodist Church at the time of the writer's retirement.

I review the years of my life, I am possessed by an overwhelming sense of my inexpressible debt to my Heavenly Father, my church, and my companions of the way. Memory confronts me with the knowledge of God's forgiving mercy, sustaining grace, providential leadership, and kindly disciplines. In the presence of such redeeming love and divine guidance, thankfulness ceases to be a duty and becomes a delight. Somewhere in an Italian garden there is an ancient sundial inscribed with this motto, "I record only the sunny hours." In that spirit I desire to record my sentiments as I approach the hour of my official retirement.

Gratitude is the mother of all virtues and it springs from an awareness of God's goodness to us. About the only offering I have to make to God is a thankful heart; so I join with the Psalmist in saying:

> Bless the Lord, O my soul,
> and forget not all his benefits.

More than half a century has slipped by since the hour in which I dedicated my life to Christ and answered the call to the ministry. These years have been crowded with happy privileges, staggering responsibilities, and an innumerable company of rewarding friends. As I approach the time of my retirement, the emotions of my heart and mind are like those aroused when looking through an old album of photographs, every page of which mirrors cherished friends and happy days. The years have placed upon my nose a pair of spectacles, and as I look through them, a rosy haze seems to color the lens. Life has been good to me. God's mercy has beleaguered my life, and the church has granted to me many privileges and honors, the least of which I have neither merited nor deserved.

Recently I read of a lady who walked into a tree and when asked how she happened to do so, replied, "I saw it, but I did not realize it." The countless blessings of my life have always been in my thoughts, but in these later years I have been made to "realize" them more than ever. More time and space than are available would be required for me to enumerate these blessings. Out of the multitude, let me mention—yes, inscribe in indelible ink—at least seven of God's gracious gifts.

I. I REMEMBER
My Christian Home

My good father and mother were devout in their faith, simple in their tastes, and faithful in the fulfillment of all the obligations laid upon sincere Christians and patriotic citizens. Into that economically poor but devout and happy home, I was born. We lacked much of this world's goods, but we were rich and happy in love and contentment. These dear parents bequeathed to me a heritage of faith and courage which in all subsequent years has enriched and strengthened my life.

When I think of my parents, I am reminded that on both sides of my family disciplined, cultivated, and courageous living has gone into my making. A part of the wisdom of life is to discover that in its journey some things are so precious we cannot afford to leave them behind. For me they include the recollections of my childhood home, the voices of the preachers who ministered to me in my youth, and directed the thoughts of a growing boy on things divine. Though my parents and these dear preachers have long since fallen to sleep, the memory of them is for me a perpetual source of inspiration and uplift. I walk with braver step, stronger faith, and larger hope because of their faith and guidance.

II. I REMEMBER
The Constraint Christ Laid upon My Life

Although there were stirrrings of religious interest in my boyhood years, there was also indifference and careless living. As a young man of twenty-one, under the spiritual guidance of my dear wife and the winsome invitation of a preacher of righteousness, I sought the Lord, and he embraced me in his arms of measureless mercy and whispered that my sins were forgiven. Almost immediately following my conversion came his call to the Christian ministry. When I heard him say, "Whom shall I send?" I answered, "Here am I, send me." Although I had nothing to offer as fitness for the high calling of the ministry, he called and I answered. His voice sounded louder than my own self-interests, and I determined to put his cause above my comfort. For more than half a century the cry of needy lands and sinning humanity has been my major concern, and yet when I look at the fruits of my ministry, I feel ashamed for so much has gone undone. But humbly I do claim that my ministry has been Christ-centered and that I have always sought so to exalt Christ that men would be drawn to him.

III. I REMEMBER
The Incredible Good News of the Gospel
I Have Been Privileged to Proclaim

I would be the last one to claim any worthiness for the Christian ministry. There has always been before me an unattainable, ever-receding goal. My dreams and my deeds have not always matched. If one of the requirements for being a preacher were a sense of worthiness, I could never attempt another sermon. There are goals in spiritual attainment one always seeks, but never fully apprehends. I have been comforted when I remembered that Christianity is not a religion that advertises human goodness, but one that proclaims God's marvelous grace and everlasting mercy. I do know that, through all the changing years of my life, there has been an unbroken thread of God's guidance that has given saving significance to what little I have been able to accomplish.

138

Immediately following my conversion, I decided the kind of preacher I wanted to be. Like all of my ideals, this one has outrun my accomplishments, but it is a torch that has burned steadily before the eyes of my soul. I have always wanted my preaching to deal with the central certainties of our faith. My prayer has been that I might be a faithful messenger of the gladdest news that ever broke upon the ears of men. Good news about the Savior and his power to forgive sin! Good news about the triumph of righteousness and the coming of the kingdom of God! Good news about the transfiguration of sorrow and the withering of the bitter roots of anxiety! Good news about the stingless death and the triumphant certainty of life after death!

Through all these years the preaching of the unsearchable riches of Christ has been my highest joy. I have yet to find a combination of words which fully expresses the deep convictions of my heart concerning Christ. Service in the Christian ministry has been for me a happy experience. The optimism and daring of youth have given way to the settled and satisfying faith of more mature years, but Christ continues to monopolize the sky of my life and the passing of the years brings deeper knowledge of his presence and power. I am fully convinced that, apart from Christ, the world lies in darkness and despair and that only in him can men find salvation, sanity, safety, or satisfaction. He alone has the solution of the world's problems. If the fondest dreams and the highest hopes of mankind are ever fulfilled, it will be in obedience to his will.

> He wakes desires you never may forget,
> He shows you stars you never saw before,
> He makes you share with Him for evermore
> The burden of the world's divine regret.

How wise you were to open not! and yet
How poor if you should turn Him from the door! [1]

IV. I REMEMBER
The Friends God Has Given Me

Next to the mercy of God and the influence of my family, I place the friends with whom I have walked in the way. In recent years I have found myself lingering lovingly upon their names; they have been with me in many hours and many circumstances. Some of them have passed through the gates eternal and are at home in God's house; yet many remain on this side of the river, and the privilege of standing beside them puts iron into my blood and courage into my soul. Many have been my brother preachers, many have been devout laymen, many are in lands across the seas. Friends such as these make heaven necessary and immortality compulsory, In that country where God lets us reside when the sun goes down in our west, where long shadows never darken, I shall live with this gracious company and be happy there as I have been here.

V. I REMEMBER
How Good The Methodist Church Has Been to Me

The Methodist Church has laid upon my shoulders many responsibilities, but it has also given to me a great many honors. Perhaps no man ever stood seeking admission at the bar of an Annual Conference with so little to offer as credentials of his worthiness for the work of the ministry. But in great kindness, the South Georgia Conference received me "on trial" in 1909. From that humble circuit to which I was sent in that year, I have traveled a worldwide circuit and had the privilege of being the "ambassador" of Methodism upon almost every continent of the earth.

[1] From *The Vitality of Faith* by Murdo E. Macdonald (Nashville: Abingdon Press, 1956), p. 120.

Much of my ministry has been outside these United States—some of it in far and difficult places where I labored in tempestuous times. There I saw the organized forces of evil unfurl their banners and put their armies in battle formation against the church, but I have never doubted the final triumph of righteousness. It never occurred to me that the church was in a battle that might be lost, but rather that it was in the service of the King Triumphant. Whenever I have gone and with whomsoever I have labored, the great and the unknown, I have coveted no higher title than that of "Methodist preacher."

VI. I REMEMBER

The Certainties of My Faith Which Time Has Not Dimmed

The supreme aim of my ministry has been to witness and to share. At the beginning I was told that a Methodist preacher was supposed to be a "man with an experience to share and a story to tell." Preaching, therefore, has been both a sacred duty and a great joy. I have humbly taken my stand with those who gratefully and joyfully accept and proclaim the doctrines historically associated with evangelical Christianity. Doubt begets no enthusiasm and unbelief sends no missionaries. I am convinced that our distraught world does not seek a new definition of religion but a new realization of Christ's power. Men are asking, not for speculation, but for the spectacle of men who manifest in their preaching and living a quenchless love for souls. If, by my inadequate telling of the story of Jesus and his love, I have led some of the knowledge of Christ and brightened the hope of the saints, I have not lived in vain.

When John cried, "Behold, the Lamb of God," he was asserting the finality of Christ. Religion is nothing unless it deserves unconditional dedication; unless we can rest ourselves upon it in life and death, it is not adequate. For me the evidences of Christ's unrivaled

141

greatness are steadily growing. One does not have to search the writings of men for the most thrilling and romantic message ever spoken to man. It is written in the New Testament, when it speaks to us of the unceasing love of God and the adequate redemption offered in Christ. To follow Christ is to face the future, not only without despair, but with undecaying hope. In the risen Christ we find the lifting of the shadow and the loosening of our bonds. If our faith cannot stand squarely before all of its critics in full conviction of its authenticity, and so stand without fear or apology, we have no gospel to preach. We need to behold Christ on his triumphant march through history, and despite the tumult of our fevered day, submit our wills to his law and our souls to his cleansing. The passing of the years has brought to me a rediscovery of this blessed truth, and I understand better with each passing day what Peter meant when he said, "You have the words of eternal life."

VII. I REMEMBER
The Land Where Someday I Shall Live with Him

God has set the eternal in our hearts. He makes the seen and the unseen one. He bridges the gulf between a world that now is and the eternal world of abiding beauty. We are neither guests of a night nor captives of a cruel world, but children in the family of God. That broken sepulcher in Joseph's garden assures us that God has set the light of immortality in our hearts and not even death can put it out. Our Christian faith is never so confident, never so triumphant as when it proclaims the everlasting life. We march, not toward the setting sun, but toward the light of morning, the light "that shineth more and more unto the perfect day." This life and the next are one, and what God has joined together, let not man put asunder.

Finally, brethren, I think one and all for their patience, cooperation, and kindness. As long as I have breath, I shall be watching the growth and activity of our beloved church. To have spent so many years of my ministry in the state where I was born and bred, to have served for twenty eventful years as the presiding bishop over the Annual Conferences of my home state is an honor about which I shall speak to my children's children. While duties have literally carried me to the ends of the earth, my love for and pride in the people of Georgia have deepened.

I face retirement with a strange sort of eagerness and yet I suppose I will not fully understand what it means until I have tried it. Different people contemplate retirement in different ways; some think of it as life in a rocking chair with feet permanently propped up before a warm fire. I do not. To be honest, I do relish some release from the marching orders under which I have gone for many years. It will be a satisfaction to be free from the incessant and straining demands of administrative duties. I shall be happy to have more time with my family, to walk in a garden, read some good books, and gaze sometimes at cloudless skies. But I realize that there is danger in such lovely and leisurely contemplations as these. I fear that without some work to do I cannot be completely happy. I want to finish my ministry as I began it, confronting men with the claims and challenges of Christ.

The hour in which we live demands of us an attitude of eager expectancy and obedience. We must shake ourselves free from the apathy of a long period of difficulty. No ebb and flow of the tides of history can ever cancel or modify the command of Christ to go and preach the gospel. The church needs many things, but above all else it needs dedicated men who will set the trumpet of the everlasting gospel to their lips and proclaim the all-sufficiency of Christ. The light that falls upon our pathway is not the light of the setting sun. It is the light of the morning.

My prayer for you who comprise the membership of this conference, both now and in the future, is that you may keep the banners of your faith flying so high that others may be made brave and come to stand at your side. To do so you must bend your strength to the cultivation of the deep places of the soul. You must practice a Christianity so effectively and redemptively in contact with the agony of our times that men cannot but say in their hearts, "Here is hope; here is salvation." If we lose our overmastering consciousness of God and the solemn sense of our responsibility to him, then we have lost our hope for man's redemption and our expectation of a society in which human aspirations can be disciplined and given fulfillment. Without the ideals and restraints of Christ's gospel, people become thoughtless and life is an irrational existence. There is no salvation for men and no hope for our civilization if we fail to follow him who is the Way, the Truth and the Life.

> Let me but live my life from year to year,
>> With forward face and unreluctant soul;
>> Not hurrying to, nor turning from, the goal;
> Not mourning for the things that disappear
> In the dim past, nor holding back in fear
>> From what the future veils; but with a whole
>> And happy heart, that pays its toll
> To Youth and Age, and travels on with cheer.
>
> So let the way wind up the hill or down,
>> O'er rough or smooth, the journey will be joy;
>> Still seeking what I sought when but a boy,
> New friendships, high adventure, and a crown,
>> My heart will keep the courage of the quest,
>> And hope the road's last turn will be the best.[2]
>   —HENRY VAN DYKE

[2] "Life" by Henry van Dyke. Used by permission of Charles Scribner's Son.